FOR THE LIFE OF THE WORLD

FOR THE LIFE
OF THE WORLD
Sacraments and Orthodoxy

by
ALEXANDER SCHMEMANN

ST VLADIMIR'S SEMINARY PRESS
CRESTWOOD, NEW YORK

LIBRARY OF CONGRESS CATALOGING-IN-PUBLICATION DATA

Schmemann, Alexander, 1921-1983
    For the life of the world.
    Rev. and expanded ed. of: Sacraments and orthodoxy, 1965.
    Includes bibliographical references.
    1. Orthodox Eastern Church—Liturgy. 2. Sacraments—Orthodox
Eastern Church. I. Title.

BX350.S36   1982   264'.019   82-17033
ISBN 0-913836-08-7

ST VLADIMIR'S SEMINARY PRESS
575 Scarsdale Rd, Crestwood, New York 10707-1699
1-800-204-2665
www.svspress.com

Copyright © 1963,
copyright © revised edition 1973
by Alexander Schmemann

First edition 1963
Second, revised and expanded edition 1973

ISBN 978-0-913836-08-8

PRINTED IN THE UNITED STATES OF AMERICA

Contents

Preface

This little book was written ten years ago as a "study guide" to the Quadrennial Conference of the National Student Christian Federation held in Athens, Ohio, in December 1963. It was not meant to be and it is certainly not a systematic theological treatise of the Orthodox liturgical tradition. My only purpose in writing it was to outline—to students preparing themselves for a discussion of Christian mission—the Christian "world view," i.e., the approach to the world and to man's life in it that stems from the liturgical experience of the Orthodox Church.

It so happened however, that the book reached a readership far beyond the student circles for which it was written. Reprinted in 1965 by Herder and Herder (under the title *Sacraments and Orthodoxy*), then in England *(World As Sacrament)*, translated into French, Italian and Greek, it was even recently "published" in an anonymous Russian translation by the underground *samizdat* in the Soviet Union. All this proves, I am sure, not any particular qualities of the book itself—more than anyone I am aware of its many defects and insufficiencies—but the importance of the issue which I tried to deal with and whose urgency, evident ten years ago, is even more evident today and the only justification for this new edition.

These issues are none other than *secularism*—the progressive and rapid alienation of our culture, of its very foundations, from the Christian experience and "world view" which initially shaped that culture—and the deep polarization which secularism has provoked among Christians themselves. Indeed, while some seem to welcome secularism as the best fruit of Christianity in history, some others find in it the justification for an almost Manichean rejection of the world, for an escape into a disincarnate and dualistic "spirituality." Thus there are those who reduce the Church to the world and its problems, and those who simply equate the world with evil and morbidly rejoice in their apocalyptic gloom.

Both attitudes distort, I am convinced, the wholeness, the *catholicity* of the genuine Orthodox tradition which has always affirmed both the *goodness* of the world for whose life God has given his only-begotten Son, and the *wickedness* in which the world lies, which has always proclaimed and keeps proclaiming every Sunday that "by the Cross joy has entered the world," yet tells those who believe in Christ that they "are dead and their life is hid with Christ in God" (Col. 3:3).

And thus our real question is: how can we "hold together"—in faith, in life, in action—these seemingly contradictory affirmations of the Church, how can we overcome the temptation to opt for and to "absolutize" one of them, falling thus into the wrong choices or "heresies" that have so often plagued Christianity in the past?

It is my certitude that the answer comes to us not from neat intellectual theories, but above all from that living and unbroken experience of the Church which she reveals and communicates to us in her worship, in the *leitourgia* always making her that which she is: the sacrament of the world, the sacrament of the Kingdom—their gift to us *in Christ*. And it is this experience that I tried, not so much to explain or to analyse, but rather simply to *confirm* in this essay.

Had I to write it today I would have probably written it differently. But I do not believe in, nor am I capable of, rewriting that which was written once, however imperfectly, with the whole heart. Therefore only a few minor corrections and alterations were made in this reprint. I have also added, in the form of appendices, two essays written in a somewhat different "key" but which may help, I hope, better to understand some of the implications of this book.

Finally I would like to use the opportunity given me

by this new edition to express my deep gratitude to those whose reactions to my work were for me the source of great joy: to Mr. Zissimos Lorenzatos of Athens who, of his own initiative, simply because, as he wrote to me, he "felt he must do it," published a magnificent Greek translation of this book; to my unknown friends in Russia: learning of their humble, typewritten edition of my essay was one of the most moving experiences of my life; to all those who wrote to me and whose messages were for me the joyful affirmation of our unity "in faith and love"; last but not least, to my friends David Drillock and Anthony Pluth who spared no effort in preparing this new edition.

January, 1973   —*Alexander Schmemann*

1

The Life of the World

"Man is what he eats." With this statement the German materialistic philosopher Feuerbach thought he had put an end to all "idealistic" speculations about human nature. In fact, however, he was expressing, without knowing it, the most religious idea of man. For long before Feuerbach the same definition of man was given by the Bible. In the biblical story of creation man is presented, first of all, as a hungry being, and the whole world as his food. Second only to the direction to propagate and have dominion over the earth, according to the author of the first chapter of Genesis, is God's instruction to men to eat of the earth: "Behold I have given you every herb bearing seed . . . and every tree, which is the fruit of a tree yielding seed; to you it shall be for meat. . . ." Man must eat in order to live; he must take the world into his body and transform it into himself, into flesh and blood. He is indeed that which he eats, and the whole world is presented as one all-embracing banquet table for man. And this image of the banquet remains, throughout the whole Bible, the central image of life. It is the image of life at its creation and also the image of life at its end and fulfillment: ". . . that you eat and drink at my table in my Kingdom."

I begin with this seemingly secondary theme of food— secondary from the standpoint of the great "religious issues" of our time—because the very purpose of this essay is to answer, if possible, the question: of what life do we speak, what life do we preach, proclaim and announce when, as Christians, we confess that Christ died for the life of the world? What *life* is both motivation, and the beginning and the goal of Christian *mission?*

The existing answers follow two general patterns. There are those among us for whom life, when discussed in religious terms, means *religious life.* And this religious life is a world in itself, existing apart from the secular world and its life. It is the world of "spirituality," and in our days it seems to gain more and more popularity. Even the airport bookstands are filled with anthologies of mystical writings. *Basic Mysticism* is a title we saw on one of them. Lost and confused in the noise, the rush and the frustrations of "life," man easily accepts the invitation to enter into the inner sanctuary of his soul and to discover there another life, to enjoy a "spiritual banquet" amply supplied with spiritual food. This spiritual food will *help* him. It will help him to restore his peace of mind, to endure the other—the secular—life, to accept its tribulations, to lead a wholesome and more dedicated life, to "keep smiling" in a deep, religious way. And thus *mission* consists here in converting people to this "spiritual" life, in making them "religious."

There exists a great variety of emphases and even theologies within this general pattern, from the popular revival to the sophisticated interest in esoteric mystical doctrines. But the result is the same: "religious" life makes the secular one—the life of eating and drinking—irrelevant, deprives it of any real meaning save that of being an exercise in piety and patience. And the more spiritual is the "religious banquet," the more secular and material become the neon lighted signs EAT, DRINK that we see along our highways.

But there are those also, to whom the affirmation "for the life of the world" seems to mean naturally "for the *better* life of the world." The "spiritualists" are counterbalanced by the activists. To be sure we are far today from the simple optimism and euphoria of the "Social Gospel." All the implications of existentialism with its anxieties, of neo-Orthodoxy with its pessimistic and realistic view of history, have been assimilated and given proper consideration. But the fundamental belief in Christianity as being first of all *action* has remained intact, and in fact has acquired a new strength. From this point of view Christianity has simply lost the world. And the world must be recovered. The Christian mission, therefore, is to catch up with the life that has gone astray. The "eating" and "drinking" man is taken quite seriously, almost too seriously. He constitutes the virtually exclusive object of Christian action, and we are constantly called to repent for having spent too much time in contemplation and adoration, in silence and liturgy, for having not dealt sufficiently with the social, political, economic, racial and all other issues of real life. To books on mysticism and spirituality correspond books on "Religion and *Life*" (or *Society*, or *Urbanism* or *Sex* . . .). And yet the basic question remains unanswered: what is this *life* that we must regain for Christ and make Christian? What is, in other words, the ultimate end of all this doing and action?

Suppose we have reached at least one of these practical goals, have "won"—then what? The question may seem a naive one, but one cannot really act without knowing the meaning not only of action, but of the life itself in the name of which one acts. One eats and drinks, one fights for freedom and justice in order to be *alive,* to have the *fullness of life.* But what is it? What is the life of life itself? What is the content of life eternal? At some ultimate point, within some ultimate analysis, we inescapably discover that in and by itself action has no meaning. When all committees have fulfilled their task, all papers have been distributed and all practical goals achieved, there must come a perfect joy. About what? Unless we know, the same dichotomy between religion and life, which we have observed in the spiritual solution, remains. Whether we "spiritualize" our life or "secularize" our religion, whether we invite men to a spiritual banquet or simply join them at the secular one, the real life of the world, for which we are told God gave his only-begotten Son, remains hopelessly beyond our religious grasp.

2

"Man is what he eats." But what does he eat and why? These questions seem naive and irrelevant not only to Feuerbach. They seemed even more irrelevant to his religious opponents. To them, as to him, eating was a material function, and the only important question was whether in addition to it man possessed a spiritual "superstructure." Religion said yes. Feuerbach said no. But both answers were given within the same fundamental opposition of the spiritual to the material. "Spiritual" *versus* "material," "sacred" *versus* "profane," "supernatural" *versus* "natural"—such were for centuries the only accepted, the only understandable moulds and categories of religious thought and experience. And Feuerbach, for all his materialism, was in fact a natural heir to Christian "idealism" and "spiritualism."

But the Bible, we have seen, also begins with man as a hungry being, with the man who is that which he eats. The perspective, however, is wholly different, for nowhere in the Bible do we find the dichotomies which for us are the self-evident framework of all approaches to religion. In the Bible the food that man eats, the world of which he must partake in order to live, is given to him by God, and it is given as *communion with God*. The world as man's food is not something "material" and limited to material functions, thus different from, and opposed to, the specifically "spiritual" functions by which man is related to God. All that exists is God's gift to man, and it all exists to make God known to man, to make man's life communion with God. It is divine love made food, made life for man. God *blesses* everything He creates, and, in biblical language, this means that He makes all creation the sign and means of His presence and wisdom, love and revelation: "O taste and see that the Lord is good."

Man is a hungry being. But he is hungry for God. Behind all the hunger of our life is God. All desire is finally a desire for Him. To be sure, man is not the only hungry being. All that exists lives by "eating." The whole creation depends on food. But the unique position of man in the universe is that

he alone is to *bless* God for the food and the life he receives
from Him. He alone is to respond to God's blessing with
his blessing. The significant fact about the life in the Garden is that man is to *name* things. As soon as animals have
been created to keep Adam company, God brings them to
Adam to see what he will call them. "And whatsoever Adam
called every living creature, that was the name thereof."
Now, in the Bible a name is infinitely more than a means to
distinguish one thing from another. It reveals the very essence of a thing, or rather its essence as God's gift. To
name a thing is to manifest the meaning and value God
gave it, to know it as coming from God and to know its
place and function within the cosmos created by God.

To name a thing, in other words, is to bless God for it
and in it. And in the Bible to bless God is not a "religious"
or a "cultic" act, but the very *way of life*. God blessed the
world, blessed man, blessed the seventh day (that is, time),
and this means that He filled all that exists with His love
and goodness. made all this "very good." So the only
natural (and not "supernatural") reaction of man, to whom
God gave this blessed and sanctified world, is to bless God
in return, to thank Him, to *see* the world as God sees it
and—in this act of gratitude and adoration—to know, name
and possess the world. All rational, spiritual and other
qualities of man, distinguishing him from other creatures,
have their focus and ultimate fulfillment in this capacity to
bless God, to know, so to speak, the meaning of the thirst
and hunger that constitutes his life. "*Homo sapiens*," "*homo
faber*" . . . yes, but, first of all, "*homo adorans*." The first,
the basic definition of man is that he is *the priest*. He stands
in the center of the world and unifies it in his act of blessing
God, of both receiving the world from God and offering
it to God—and by filling the world with this eucharist, he
transforms his life, the one that he receives from the world,
into life in God, into communion with Him. The world
was created as the "matter," the material of one all-embracing
eucharist, and man was created as the priest of this cosmic
sacrament.

Men understand all this instinctively if not rationally.

Centuries of secularism have failed to transform eating into something strictly utilitarian. Food is still treated with reverence. A meal is still a rite—the last "natural sacrament" of family and friendship, of life that is more than "eating" and "drinking." To eat is still something more than to maintain bodily functions. People may not understand what that "something more" is, but they nonetheless desire to celebrate it. They are still hungry and thirsty for sacramental life.

3

It is not accidental, therefore, that the biblical story of the Fall is centered again on food. Man ate the forbidden fruit. The fruit of that one tree, whatever else it may signify, was unlike every other fruit in the Garden: it was not offered as a gift to man. Not given, not blessed by God, it was food whose eating was condemned to be communion with itself alone, and not with God. It is the image of the world loved for itself, and eating it is the image of life understood as an end in itself.

To love is not easy, and mankind has chosen not to return God's love. Man has loved the world, but as an end in itself and not as transparent to God. He has done it so consistently that it has become something that is "in the air." It seems natural for man to experience the world as opaque, and not shot through with the presence of God. It seems natural not to live a life of thanksgiving for God's gift of a world. It seems natural not to be eucharistic.

The world is a fallen world because it has fallen away from the awareness that God is all in all. The accumulation of this disregard for God is the original sin that blights the world. And even the religion of this fallen world cannot heal or redeem it, for it has accepted the reduction of God to an area called "sacred" ("spiritual," "supernatural")—as opposed to the world as "profane." It has accepted the all-embracing secularism which attempts to steal the world away from God.

The natural dependence of man upon the world was intended to be transformed constantly into communion with God in whom is all life. Man was to be the priest of a eucharist, offering the world to God, and in this offering he was to receive the gift of life. But in the fallen world man does not have the priestly power to do this. His dependence on the world becomes a closed circuit, and his love is deviated from its true direction. He still loves, he is still hungry. He knows he is dependent on that which is beyond him. But his love and his dependence refer only to the world in itself. He does not know that breathing can be communion with God. He does not realize that to eat can be to receive life from God in more than its physical sense. He forgets that the world, its air or its food cannot by themselves bring life, but only as they are received and accepted for God's sake, in God and as bearers of the divine gift of life. By themselves they can produce only the appearance of life.

When we see the world as an end in itself, everying becomes itself a value and consequently loses all value, because only in God is found the meaning (value) of everything, and the world is meaningful only when it is the "sacrament" of God's presence. Things treated merely as things in themselves destroy themselves because only in God have they any life. The world of nature, cut off from the source of life, is a dying world. For one who thinks food in itself is the source of life, eating is communion with the dying world, it is communion with death. Food itself is dead, it is life that has died and it must be kept in refrigerators like a corpse.

For "the wages of sin is death." The life man chose was only the appearance of life. God showed him that he himself had decided to eat bread in a way that would simply return him to the ground from which both he and the bread had been taken: "For dust thou art and into dust shalt thou return." Man lost the eucharistic life, he lost the life of life itself, the power to transform it into Life. He ceased to be the priest of the world and became its slave.

In the story of the Garden this took place in the cool of

the day: that is, at night. And Adam, when he left the Garden where life was to have been eucharistic—an offering of the world in thanksgiving to God—Adam led the whole world, as it were, into darkness. In one of the beautiful pieces of Byzantine hymnology Adam is pictured sitting outside, facing Paradise, weeping. It is the figure of man himself.

4

We can interrupt here for a while this theme of food. We began with it only in order to free the terms "sacramental" and "eucharistic" from the connotations they have acquired in the long history of technical theology, where they are applied almost exclusively within the framework of "natural" *versus* "supernatural," and "sacred" *versus* "profane," that is, within the same opposition between religion and life which makes life ultimately unredeemable and religiously meaningless. In our perspective, however, the "original" sin is not primarily that man has "disobeyed" God; the sin is that he ceased to be hungry for Him and for Him alone, ceased to see his whole life depending on the whole world as a sacrament of communion with God. The sin was not that man neglected his religious duties. The sin was that he thought of God in terms of religion, i.e., opposing Him to life. The only real fall of man is his noneucharistic life in a noneucharistic world. The fall is not that he preferred world to God, distorted the balance between the spiritual and material, but that he made the world *material*, whereas he was to have transformed it into "life in God," filled with meaning and spirit.

But it is the Christian gospel that God did not leave man in his exile, in the predicament of confused longing. He had created man "after his own heart" and for Himself, and man has struggled in his freedom to find the answer to the mysterious hunger in him. In this scene of radical unfulfillment God acted decisively: into the darkness where man was groping toward Paradise, He sent light. He did so

not as a rescue operation, to recover lost man: it was rather
for the completing of what He had undertaken from the
beginning. God acted so that man might understand who
He really was and where his hunger had been driving him.

The light God sent was his Son: the same light that had
been shining unextinguished in the world's darkness all
along, seen now in full brightness.

Before Christ came, God had promised Him to man. He
had done so in major fashion, speaking through the prophets of Israel, but also in those many other ways in which He
communicates with man. As Christians we believe that He,
who is the truth about both God and man, gives foretastes
of His incarnation in all more fragmentary truths. We believe as well that Christ is present in any seeker after truth.
Simone Weil has said that though a person may run as fast as
he can away from Christ, if it is toward what he considers
true, he runs in fact straight into the arms of Christ.

Much that is true of God has also been revealed in the
long history of religion, and this can be demonstrated for
the Christian by reference to the true standard of Christ. In
the great religions which have given shape to human aspirations, God plays on an orchestra which is far out of tune,
yet there has often been a marvelous, rich music made.

Christianity, however, is in a profound sense the *end of
all religion*. In the Gospel story of the Samaritan woman at
the well, Jesus made this clear. " 'Sir,' the woman said to
him, 'I perceive that thou art a prophet. Our fathers worshipped in this mountain; and ye say, that in Jerusalem is
the place where men ought to worship.' Jesus saith unto her,
'Woman, believe me, the hour cometh, when ye shall neither
in this mountain, nor yet at Jerusalem, worship the
Father. . . . But the hour cometh, and now is, when the
true worshippers shall worship the Father in spirit and in
truth: for the Father seeketh such to worship him' " (Jn.
4:19—21, 23). She asked him a question about cult, and in
reply Jesus changed the whole perspective of the matter.
Nowhere in the New Testament, in fact, is Christianity
presented as a cult or as a religion. Religion is needed where
there is a wall of separation between God and man. But

Christ who is both God and man has broken down the wall between man and God. He has inaugurated a new life, not a new religion.

It was this freedom of the early church from "religion" in the usual, traditional sense of this word that led the pagans to accuse Christians of *atheism*. Christians had no concern for any sacred geography, no temples, no cult that could be recognized as such by the generations fed with the solemnities of the mystery cults. There was no specific religious interest in the places where Jesus had lived. There were no pilgrimages. The old religion had its thousand sacred places and temples: for the Christians all this was past and gone. There was no need for temples built of stone: Christ's Body, the Church itself, the new people gathered in Him, was the only real temple. "Destroy ·this temple, and in three days I will raise it up. . . ." (Jn. 2:19).

The Church itself was the new and heavenly Jerusalem: the Church *in* Jerusalem was by contrast unimportant. The fact that Christ *comes* and is *present* was far more significant than the places where He had been. The historical reality of Christ was of course the undisputed ground of the early Christians' faith: yet they did not so much remember Him as know He was with them. And in Him was the end of "religion," because He himself was the Answer to all religion, to all human hunger for God, because in Him the life that was lost by man—and which could only be symbolized, signified, asked for in religion—was restored to man.

5

This is not a treatise of systematic theology. It does not attempt to explore all the aspects and implications of this Answer. Nor does it pretend to add anything—in this small scope—to the wisdom accumulated in innumerable volumes of "theologies" and "dogmatics." The purpose of this book is a humble one. It is to remind its readers that in Christ, life—life in all its totality—was returned to man, given again as sacrament and communion, made Eucharist. And it is to show—be it only partially and superficially—the meaning of this for our mission in the world. The Western Christian is used to thinking of sacrament as opposed to the Word, and he links the mission with the Word and not the sacrament. He is, moreover, accustomed to consider the sacrament as perhaps an essential and clearly defined part or institution or act *of* the Church and *within* the Church, but not of the Church as being itself the sacrament of Christ's presence and action. And finally he is primarily interested in certain very "formal" questions concerning the sacraments: their number, their "validity," their institution, etc. Our purpose is to show that there exists and always existed a different perspective, a different approach to sacrament, and that this approach may be of crucial importance precisely for the whole burning issue of mission, of our witness to Christ in the world. For the basic question is: *of what are we witnesses?* What have we seen and touched with our hands? Of what have we partaken and been made communicants? Where do we call men? What can we offer them?

This essay is written by an Orthodox and in the perspective of the Orthodox Church. But it is not a book about Orthodoxy, as the books about Orthodoxy are written and understood today. There exists a "Western" approach to the East which the Orthodox themselves have accepted. Orthodoxy is presented usually as specializing in "mysticism" and "spirituality," as the potential home of all those who thirst and hunger for the "spiritual banquet." The Orthodox Church has been assigned the place and the function of the "liturgical" and "sacramental" Church, *therefore* more or less indifferent to mission. But all this is wrong. The Orthodox may have failed much too often to see the real implications of their "sacramentalism," but its fundamental meaning is certainly not that of escaping into a timeless "spirituality" far from the dull world of "action." And it is this true meaning that this writer would like to disclose and share with his readers.

Beautiful churches with "all night vigil services," icons and processions, a liturgy which to be properly performed requires not less than twenty-seven heavy liturgical books—

all this seems to contradict what has been said above about Christianity as the "end of religion." But does it in fact? And if not, what is the *meaning* of all this in the real world in which we live, and for the life of which God has given His Son?

2

The Eucharist

In this world Christ was rejected. He was the perfect expression of life as God intended it. The fragmentary life of the world was gathered into His life; He was the heart beat of the world and the world killed Him. But in that murder the world itself died. It lost its last chance to become the paradise God created it to be. We can go on developing new and better material things. We can build a more humane society which may even keep us from annihilating each other. But when Christ, the true life of the world, was rejected, it was the beginning of the end. That rejection had a finality about it: He was crucified for good. As Pascal said: "Christ is in agony until the end of the world."

Christianity often appears, however, to preach that if men will try hard enough to live Christian lives, the crucifixion can somehow be reversed. This is because Christianity has forgotten itself, forgotten that always it must first of all stand at the cross. Not that this world cannot be improved—one of our goals is certainly to work for peace, justice, freedom. But while it can be improved, it can never become the place God intended it to be. Christianity does not condemn the world. The world has condemned itself when on Calvary it condemned the One who was its true self. "He was in the world, and the world was made by him, and the world knew him not" (Jn. 1:10). If we think seriously about the real meaning, the real scope of these words, we *know* that as Christians and insofar as we are Christians we are, first of all, witnesses of that *end*: end of all natural joy; end of all satisfaction of man with the world and with himself; end, indeed, of life itself as a reasonable and reasonably organized "pursuit of happiness." Christians did not have to wait for the modern proponents of existentialist anxiety, despair and absurdity to be aware of all this. And although in the course of their long history Christians have much too often forgotten the meaning of the cross, and enjoyed life as if "nothing had happened," although each one of us too often takes "time off"—we know that in the world in which Christ died, "natural life" has been brought to its end.

2

And yet, from its very beginning Christianity has been the proclamation of joy, of the only possible joy on earth. It rendered impossible all joy we usually think of as possible. But within this impossibility, at the very bottom of this darkness, it announced and conveyed a new all-embracing joy, and with this joy it transformed the End into a Beginning. Without the proclamation of this joy Christianity is incomprehensible. It is only as joy that the Church was victorious in the world, and it lost the world when it lost that joy, and ceased to be a credible witness to it. Of all accusations against Christians, the most terrible one was uttered by Nietzsche when he said that Christians had no joy.

Let us, therefore, forget for a while the technical discussions about the Church, its mission, its methods. Not that these discussions are wrong or unnecessary—but they can be useful and meaningful only within a fundamental context, and that context is the "great joy" from which everything else in Christianity developed and acquired its meaning. "For, behold, I bring you good tidings of great joy"—thus begins the Gospel, and its end is: "And they worshipped him and returned to Jerusalem with great joy." (Lk. 2:10, 24:52). And we must recover the meaning of this great joy. We must if possible partake of it, before we discuss anything

else—programs and missions, projects and techniques.
Joy, however, is not something one can define or analyze.
One enters into joy. "Enter thou into the joy of thy Lord"
(Mt. 25:21). And we have no other means of entering into
that joy, no way of understanding it, except through the
one action which from the beginning has been for the
Church both the source and the fulfillment of joy, the very
sacrament of joy, the Eucharist.

The Eucharist is a liturgy. And he who says *liturgy* today
is likely to get involved in a controversy. For to some—the
"liturgically minded"—of all the activities of the Church,
liturgy is the most important, if not the only one. To others,
liturgy is esthetic and spiritual deviation from the real
task of the Church. There exist today "liturgical" and "non-
liturgical" churches and Christians. But this controversy is
unnecessary for it has its roots in one basic misunderstanding—the "liturgical" understanding of the liturgy. This is
the reduction of the liturgy to "cultic" categories, its definition as a sacred act of worship, different as such not only
from the "profane" area of life, but even from all other
activities of the Church itself. But this is not the original
meaning of the Greek word *leitourgia*. It meant an action
by which a group of people become something corporately
which they had not been as a mere collection of individuals
—a whole greater than the sum of its parts. It meant also a
function or "ministry" of a man or of a group on behalf of
and in the interest of the whole community. Thus the
leitourgia of ancient Israel was the corporate work of a
chosen few to prepare the world for the coming of the
Messiah. And in this very act of preparation they became
what they were called to be, the Israel of God, the chosen
instrument of His purpose.

Thus the Church itself is a *leitourgia*, a ministry, a calling
to act in this world after the fashion of Christ, to bear testimony to Him and His kingdom. The eucharistic liturgy,
therefore, must not be approached and understood in
"liturgical" or "cultic" terms alone. Just as Christianity can
—and must—be considered the end of religion, so the
Christian liturgy in general, and the Eucharist in particular,

are indeed the end of cult, of the "sacred" religious act isolated from, and opposed to, the "profane" life of the community. The first condition for the understanding of liturgy
is to forget about any specific "liturgical piety."

The Eucharist is a sacrament. But he who says sacrament
also gets involved in a controversy. If we speak of sacrament, where is the Word? Are we not leading ourselves
into the dangers of "sacramentalism" and "magic," into a
betrayal of the spiritual character of Christianity? To these
questions no answer can be given at this point. For the
whole purpose of this essay is to show that the context
within which such questions are being asked is not the only
possible one. At this stage we shall say only this: the
Eucharist is the entrance of the Church into the joy of its
Lord. And to enter into that joy, so as to be a witness to it
in the world, is indeed the very calling of the Church, its
essential *leitourgia,* the sacrament by which it "becomes
what it is."

In the brief description of the Eucharist which follows,
references will be made primarily to the Orthodox eucharistic liturgy, and this for two reasons. First, in the area of
liturgy one can speak with conviction only insofar as one
has experienced that about which one is speaking. This
author's experience has been in the Orthodox tradition.
And second, it is the unanimous opinion of "liturgiologists"
that the Orthodox liturgy has best preserved those elements
and emphases which constitute the very theme of this book.

3

The liturgy of the Eucharist is best understood as a journey
or procession. It is the journey of the Church into the
dimension of the Kingdom. We use this word "dimension"
because it seems the best way to indicate the manner of our
sacramental entrance into the risen life of Christ. Color
transparencies "come alive" when viewed in three dimensions instead of two. The presence of the added dimension
allows us to see much better the actual reality of what has

been photographed. In very much the same way, though of course any analogy is condemned to fail, our *entrance* into the presence of Christ is an entrance into a fourth dimension which allows us to see the ultimate reality of life. It is not an escape from the world, rather it is the arrival at a vantage point from which we can see more deeply into the reality of the world.

The journey begins when Christians leave their homes and beds. They leave, indeed, their life in this present and concrete world, and whether they have to drive fifteen miles or walk a few blocks, a sacramental act is already taking place, an act which is the very condition of everything else that is to happen. For they are now on their way to *constitute the Church,* or to be more exact, to be transformed into the Church of God. They have been individuals, some white, some black, some poor, some rich, they have been the "natural" world and a natural community. And now they have been called to "come together in one place," to bring their lives, their very "world" with them and to be more than what they were: a *new* community with a new life. We are already far beyond the categories of common worship and prayer. The purpose of this "coming together" is not simply to add a religious dimension to the natural community, to make it "better"—more responsible, more Christian. The purpose is to *fulfill the Church,* and that means to make present the One in whom all things are at their *end,* and all things are at their *beginning.*

The liturgy begins then as a real separation from the world. In our attempt to make Christianity appeal to the man on the street, we have often minimized, or even completely forgotten, this necessary separation. We always want to make Christianity "understandable" and "acceptable" to this mythical "modern" man on the street. And we forget that the Christ of whom we speak is "not of this world," and that after His resurrection He was not recognized even by His own disciples. Mary Magdalene thought He was a gardener. When two of His disciples were going to Emmaus, "Jesus himself drew near and went with them," and they did not know Him before "he took bread, and blessed it, and brake, and gave it to them" (Lk. 24:15—16, 30). He appeared to the twelve, "the doors being shut." It was apparently no longer sufficient simply to know that He was the son of Mary. There was no physical imperative to recognize Him. He was, in other words, no longer a "part" of this world, of its reality, and to recognize Him, to enter into the joy of His presence, to be with Him, meant a conversion to another reality. The Lord's glorification does not have the compelling, objective evidence of His humiliation and cross. His glorification is known only through the mysterious death in the baptismal font, through the anointing of the Holy Spirit. It is known only in the fullness of the Church, as she gathers to meet the Lord and to share in His risen life.

The early Christians realized that in order to become the temple of the Holy Spirit they must *ascend to heaven* where Christ has ascended. They realized also that this ascension was the very condition of their mission in the world, of their ministry to the world. For there—in heaven—they were immersed in the new life of the Kingdom; and when, after this "liturgy of ascension," they returned into the world, their faces reflected the light, the "joy and peace" of that Kingdom and they were truly its witnesses. They brought no programs and no theories; but wherever they went, the seeds of the Kingdom sprouted, faith was kindled, life was transfigured, things impossible were made possible. They were witnesses, and when they were asked, "Whence shines this light, where is the source of this power?" they knew what to answer and where to lead men. In church today, we so often find we meet only the same old world, not Christ and His Kingdom. We do not realize that we never get anywhere because we never leave any place behind us.

To leave, to come. . . . This is the *beginning,* the starting point of the sacrament, the condition of its transforming power and reality.

4

The Orthodox liturgy begins with the solemn doxology: "Blessed is the Kingdom of the Father, the Son and the Holy Spirit, now and ever, and unto ages of ages." From the beginning the destination is announced: the journey is to the Kingdom. This is where we are going—and not symbolically, but really. In the language of the Bible, which is *the* language of the Church, to bless the Kingdom is not simply to acclaim it. It is to declare it to be the goal, the end of all our desires and interests, of our whole life, the supreme and ultimate value of all that exists. To bless is to accept in love, and to move toward what is loved and accepted. The Church thus is the assembly, the gathering of those to whom the ultimate destination of all life has been revealed and who have accepted it. This acceptance is expressed in the solemn answer to the doxology: Amen. It is indeed one of the most important words in the world, for it expresses the agreement of the Church to follow Christ in His ascension to His Father, to make this ascension the destiny of man. It is Christ's gift to us, for only in Him can we say Amen to God, or rather He himself is our Amen to God and the Church is an Amen to Christ. Upon this Amen the fate of the human race is decided. It reveals that the movement toward God has begun.

But we are still at the very beginning. We have left "this world." We have come together. We have heard the announcement of our ultimate destination. We have said Amen to this announcement. We are the *ecclesia,* the response to this call and order. And we begin with "common prayers and supplications," with a common and joyful act of praise. Once more, the joyful character of the eucharistic gathering must be stressed. For the medieval emphasis on the cross, while not a wrong one, is certainly one-sided. The liturgy is, before everything else, the joyous gathering of those who are to meet the risen Lord and to enter with him into the bridal chamber. And it is this joy of expectation and this expectation of joy that are expressed in singing and ritual, in vestments and in censing, in that whole "beauty" of the liturgy which has so often been denounced as unnecessary and even sinful.

Unnecessary it is indeed, for we are beyond the categories of the "necessary." Beauty is never "necessary," "functional" or "useful." And when, expecting someone whom we love, we put a beautiful tablecloth on the table and decorate it with candles and flowers, we do all this not out of necessity, but out of love. And the Church is love, expectation and joy. It is heaven on earth, according to our Orthodox tradition; it is the joy of recovered childhood, that free, unconditioned and disinterested joy which alone is capable of transforming the world. In our adult, serious piety we ask for definitions and justifications, and they are rooted in fear—fear of corruption, deviation, "pagan influences," whatnot. But "he that feareth is not made perfect in love" (1 Jn. 4:18). As long as Christians will *love* the Kingdom of God, and not only discuss it, they will "represent" it and signify it, in art and beauty. And the celebrant of the sacrament of joy will appear in a beautiful chasuble, because he is vested in the glory of the Kingdom, because even in the form of man God appears in glory. In the Eucharist we are standing in the presence of Christ, and like Moses before God, we are to be covered with his glory. Christ himself wore an unsewn garment which the soldiers at the cross did not divide: it had not been bought in the market, but in all likelihood it had been fashioned by someone's loving hands. Yes, the beauty of our preparation for the Eucharist has no practical use. But Romano Guardini has spoken wisely of this useless beauty. Of the liturgy he says:

> Man, with the aid of grace, is given the opportunity of relaying his fundamental essence, of really becoming that which according to his divine destiny he should be and longs to be, a child of God. In the liturgy he is to go "unto God, who giveth joy to his youth." . . . Because the life of the liturgy is higher than that to which customary reality gives either the opportunity or form of expression, it adapts suitable forms and methods from that sphere in which alone they are to be found, that is to say, from art. It speaks measuredly and melodiously; it employs formal, rhythmic gestures; it is clothed in colors and garments foreign to everyday life. . . . It is in the highest sense the life of a child, in which

everything is picture, melody and song. Such is the wonderful fact which the liturgy demonstrates: it unites act and reality in a supernatural childhood before God.[1]

5

The next act of the liturgy is the *entrance*: the coming of the celebrant to the altar. It has been given all possible symbolical explanations, but it is not a "symbol." It is the very movement of the Church as *passage* from the old into the new, from "this world" into the "world to come" and, as such, it is the essential movement of the liturgical "journey." In "this world" there is no altar and the temple has been destroyed. For the only altar is Christ Himself, His humanity which He has assumed and deified and made the temple of God, the altar of His presence. And Christ ascended into heaven. The altar thus is the sign that in Christ we have been given access to heaven, that the Church is the "passage" to heaven, the *entrance* into the heavenly sanctuary, and that only by "entering," by ascending to heaven does the Church fulfill herself, become what she is. And so the *entrance* at the Eucharist, this approach of the celebrant—and in him, of the whole Church—to the altar is not a symbol. It is the crucial and decisive act in which the true dimensions of the sacrament are revealed and established. It is not "grace" that comes down; it is the Church that enters into "grace," and grace means the new being, the Kingdom, the world to come. And as the celebrant approaches the altar, the Church intones the hymn which the angels eternally sing at the throne of God—"Holy God, Holy Mighty, Holy Immortal"—and the priest says: "Holy God, who art praised with the thrice holy voice of the Seraphim, glorified by the Cherubim and adored by all the hosts of heaven."

The angels are not here for decoration and inspiration. They stand precisely for heaven, for that glorious and in-

---

[1]Romano Guardini, *The Church and the Catholic, and the Spirit of the Liturgy* (New York, 1950), 180—181.

comprehensible above and beyond of which we know only one thing: that it eternally resounds with the praise of divine glory and *holiness*. "Holy" is the real name of God, of the God "not of scholars and philosophers," but of the living God of faith. The knowledge *about* God results in definitions and distinctions. The knowledge *of* God leads to this one, incomprehensible, yet obvious and inescapable word: holy. And in this word we express both that God is the Absolutely Other, the One *about* whom we know nothing, and that He is the end of all our hunger, all our desires, the inaccessible One who mobilizes our wills, the mysterious treasure that attracts us, and there is really nothing to know but Him. "Holy" is the word, the song, the "reaction" of the Church as it enters into heaven, as it stands before the heavenly glory of God.

6

Now, for the first time since the eucharistic journey began, the celebrant turns back and faces the people. Up to this moment he was the one who led the Church in its ascension, but now the movement has reached its goal. And the priest whose liturgy, whose unique function and obedience in the Church is to re-present, to make present the priesthood of Christ Himself, says to the people: "Peace be with you." In Christ man returns to God and in Christ God comes to man. As the new Adam, as the perfect man He leads us to God; as God incarnate He reveals the Father to us and reconciles us with God. He is our *peace*—the reconciliation with God, divine forgiveness, communion. And the peace that the priest announces and bestows upon us is the peace Christ has established between God and His world and into which we, the Church, have entered.

It is within this peace—"which passeth all understanding"—that now begins the liturgy of the Word. Western Christians are so accustomed to distinguish the Word from the sacrament that it may be difficult for them to understand that in the Orthodox perspective the liturgy of the

Word is as sacramental as the sacrament is "evangelical."
The sacrament is a manifestation of the Word. And unless
the false dichotomy between Word and sacrament is overcome, the true meaning of both Word and sacrament, and
especially the true meaning of Christian "sacramentalism"
cannot be grasped in all their wonderful implications. The
proclamation of the Word is a sacramental act par excellence because it is a transforming act. It transforms the
human words of the Gospel into the Word of God and the
manifestation of the Kingdom. And it transforms the man
who hears the Word into a receptacle of the Word and a
temple of the Spirit. . . . Each Saturday night, at the solemn
resurrection vigil, the book of the Gospel is brought in a
solemn procession to the midst of the congregation, and in
this act the Lord's Day is announced and manifested. For
the Gospel is not only a "record" of Christ's resurrection;
the Word of God is the eternal coming to us of the Risen
Lord, the very power and joy of the resurrection.

In the liturgy the proclamation of the Gospel is preceded
by "Alleluia," the singing of this mysterious *"theoforous"*
(God-bearing) word which is the joyful greeting of those
who *see* the coming Lord, who *know* His presence, and who
express their joy at this glorious *"parousia."* "Here He is!"
might be an almost adequate translation of this untranslatable
word.

This is why the reading and the preaching of the Gospel
in the Orthodox Church is a *liturgical act,* an integral and
essential part of the sacrament. It is heard as the Word of
God, and it is received in the Spirit—that is, in the Church,
which is the life of the Word and its "growth" in the
world.

7

Bread and wine: to understand their initial and eternal
meaning in the Eucharist we must forget for a time the
endless controversies which little by little transformed them
into "elements" of an almost abstract theological speculation.

It is indeed one of the main defects of sacramental theology that instead of following the order of the eucharistic journey with its progressive revelation of meaning, theologians applied to the Eucharist a set of abstract questions in order to squeeze it into their own intellectual framework. In this approach what virtually disappeared from the sphere of theological interest and investigation was liturgy itself, and what remained were isolated "moments," "formulas" and "conditions of validity." What disappeared was the Eucharist as one organic, all-embracing and all-transforming act of the whole Church, and what remained were "essential" and "nonessential" parts, "elements," "consecration," etc. Thus, for example, to explain and define the meaning of the Eucharist the way a certain theology does it, there is no need for the word "eucharist"; it becomes irrelevant. And yet for the early Fathers it was the key word giving unity and meaning to all the "elements" of the liturgy. The Fathers called "eucharist" the bread and wine of the offering, and their offering and consecration, and finally, communion. All this was *Eucharist* and all this could be understood only within the Eucharist.

As we proceed further in the eucharistic liturgy, the time has come now to offer to God the totality of all our lives, of ourselves, of the world in which we live. This is the first meaning of our bringing to the altar the elements of our food. For we already know that food is life, that it is the very principle of life and that the whole world has been created as food for man. We also know that to offer this food, this world, this life to God is the initial "eucharistic" function of man, his very fulfillment as man. We know that we were created as *celebrants* of the sacrament of life, of its transformation into life in God, communion with God. We know that real life is "eucharist," a movement of love and adoration toward God, the movement in which alone the meaning and the value of all that exists can be revealed and fulfilled. We know that we have lost this eucharistic life, and finally we know that in Christ, the new Adam, the perfect man, this eucharistic life was restored to man. For He Himself was the perfect Eucharist; He offered Himself in

total obedience, love and thanksgiving to God. God was His
very life. And He gave this perfect and eucharistic life to us.
In Him God became our life.

And thus this offering to God of bread and wine, of
the food that we must eat in order to live, is our offering to
Him of ourselves, of our life and of the whole world. "To
take in our hands the whole world as if it were an apple!"
said a Russian poet. It is our Eucharist. It is the movement
that Adam failed to perform, and that in Christ has become
the very life of man: a movement of adoration and praise in
which all joy and suffering, all beauty and all frustration, all
hunger and all satisfaction are referred to their ultimate
End and become finally *meaningful*. Yes, to be sure, it is a
sacrifice: but sacrifice is the most natural act of man, the
very essence of his life. Man is a sacrificial being, because he
finds his life in love, and love is sacrificial: it puts the
value, the very meaning of life in the other and gives life
to the other, and in this giving, in this sacrifice, finds the
meaning and joy of life.

We offer the world and ourselves to God. But we do it
in Christ and *in remembrance of Him*. We do it in Christ
because He has already offered all that is to be offered to
God. He has performed once and for all this Eucharist and
nothing has been left unoffered. In him was *Life*—and this
Life of all of us, He gave to God. The Church is all those
who have been accepted into the eucharistic life of Christ.
And we do it *in remembrance of Him* because, as we offer
again and again our life and our world to God, we discover
each time that there is nothing else to be offered but Christ
Himself—the Life of the world, the fullness of all that
exists. It is His Eucharist, and He is the Eucharist. As the
prayer of offering says—"it is He who offers and it is He who
is offered." The liturgy has led us into the all-embracing
Eucharist of Christ, and has revealed to us that the only
Eucharist, the only offering of the world is Christ. We
come again and again with our lives to offer; we bring and
"sacrifice"—that is, give to God—what He has given us; and
each time we come to the *End* of all sacrifices, of all offer-
ings, of all eucharist, because each time it is revealed to us

that Christ has *offered* all that exists, and that He and all
that exists has been offered in His offering of Himself. We
are included in the Eucharist of Christ and Christ is our
Eucharist.

And as the procession moves it bears the bread and wine
to the altar, and we know that it is Christ himself who takes
all of us and the totality of our life to God in His eucharistic
ascension. This is why at this moment of the liturgy we
commemorate or remember. "May the Lord God remember
in his Kingdom. . . ." Remembrance is an act of *love.* God
remembers us and His remembrance, His love is the foundation of the world. In Christ, *we remember.* We become
again beings open to love, and we *remember.* The Church
in its separation from "this world," on its journey to heaven,
remembers the world, remembers all men, remembers the
whole of creation, takes it in love to God. The Eucharist is
the sacrament of cosmic remembrance: it is indeed a restoration of love as the very life of the world.

8

The bread and wine are now on the altar, covered, hidden
as our "life is hid with Christ in God" (Col 3:3). There
lies, hidden in God, the totality of life, which Christ has
brought back to God. And the celebrant says: "Let us love
one another than in one accord we may confess. . . ." There
follows the kiss of peace, one of the fundamental acts of
Christian liturgy. The Church, if it is to be the Church,
must be the revelation of that divine Love which God
"poured out into our hearts." Without this love nothing is
"valid" in the Church because nothing is possible. The
content of Christ's Eucharist is Love, and only through
love can we enter into it and be made its partakers. Of this
love we are not capable. This love we have lost. This love
Christ has given us and this gift is the *Church.* The Church
constitutes itself through love and on love, and in this
world it is to "witness" to Love, to re-present it, to make

Love present. Love alone creates and transforms: it is, therefore, the very "principle" of the sacrament.

9

"Let us lift up our hearts," says the celebrant, and the people answer: "We have lifted them up to the Lord." The Eucharist is the *anaphora,* the "lifting up" of our offering, and of ourselves. It is the ascension of the Church to heaven. "But what do I care about heaven," says St. John Chrysostom, "when I myself have become heaven. . . ?" The Eucharist has so often been explained with reference to the gifts alone: what "happens" to bread and wine, and why, and when it happens! But we must understand that what "happens" to bread and wine happens because something has, first of all, happened to us, to the Church. It is because we have "constituted" the Church, and this means we have followed Christ in His ascension; because He has accepted us at His table in His Kingdom; because, in terms of theology, we have entered the Eschaton, and are now standing beyond time and space; it is because all this has first happened to us that something will happen to bread and wine.

"Let us lift up our hearts," says the celebrant.

"We lift them up unto the Lord," answers the congregation.

"Let us give thanks unto the Lord" (*Eucharistisomen*), says the celebrant.

10

When man stands before the throne of God, when he has fulfilled all that God has given him to fulfill, when all sins are forgiven, all joy restored, then there is nothing else for him to do but to give thanks. Eucharist (thanksgiving) is the state of perfect man. Eucharist is the life of paradise. Eucharist is the only full and real response of man to God's creation, redemption and gift of heaven. But this perfect man who stands before God is *Christ*. In Him alone all that God has given man was fulfilled and brought back to heaven. He alone is the perfect Eucharistic Being. He is the Eucharist of the world. In and through this Eucharist the whole creation becomes what it always was to be and yet failed to be.

"It is fitting and right to give thanks," answers the congregation, expressing in these words that "unconditional surrender" with which true "religion" begins. For faith is not the fruit of intellectual search, or of Pascal's "betting." It is not a reasonable solution to the frustrations and anxieties of life. It does not arise out of a "lack" of something, but ultimately it comes out of fullness, love and joy. "It is meet and right" expresses all this. It is the only possible response to the divine invitation to live and to receive abundant life.

And so the priest begins the great Eucharistic Prayer:

> It is meet and right that we should sing of Thee, bless Thee, praise Thee, give thanks unto Thee, and adore Thee in all places of Thy dominion. For Thou art God ineffable, incomprehensible, invisible, inconceivable; Thou art from everlasting and art changeless. . . . Thou from nothingness has called us into being, and when we had fallen away from Thee, Thou didst raise us again. And Thou hast not ceased to do all things until Thou hadst brought us back to heaven and endowed us with Thy Kingdom which is to come. . . . For all these things we give thanks unto Thee, for all the things whereof we know, and those whereof we know not, for all the benefits bestowed upon us, both the manifest and the unseen. . . .

This beginning of the Eucharistic Prayer is usually termed the "Preface." And although this Preface belongs to all known eucharistic rites, not much attention was given to it in the development of eucharistic theology. A "preface" is something that does not really belong to the body of a book. And theologians neglected it because they were anxious to come to the real "problems": those of consecration, the change of the elements, sacrifice, and other matters. It is here that we find the main "defect" of Christian theology; the theology of the Eucharist ceased to be eucharistic and thus took away the eucharistic spirit from the whole understanding of sacrament, from the very life of the Church. The long controversy about the words of institution and the invocation of the Holy Spirit (*epiclesis*) that went on for centuries between the East and the West is a very good example of this "noneucharistic" stage in the history of sacramental theology.

But we must understand that it is precisely this *preface* —this act, these words, this movement of thanksgiving— that really "makes possible" all that follows. For without this beginning the rest could not take place. *The Eucharist of Christ and Christ the Eucharist* is the "breakthrough" that brings us to the table in the Kingdom, raises us to heaven, and makes us partakers of the divine food. For eucharist—thanksgiving and praise—is the very form and content of the new life that God granted us when in Christ He reconciled us with Himself. The reconciliation, the forgiveness, the power of life—all this has its purpose and fulfillment in this new state of being, this new style of life which is Eucharist, the only real life of creation with God and in God, the only true relationship between God and the world.

It is indeed the *preface* to the world to come, the door into the Kingdom: and this we confess and proclaim when, speaking of the Kingdom *which is to come,* we affirm that God *has already endowed us with it.* This future has been given to us in the past that it may constitute the very *present,* the life itself, now, of the Church.

11

And thus the Preface fulfills itself in the Sanctus—the "Holy, Holy, Holy" of the eternal doxology, which is the secret essence of all that exists: "Heaven and earth are full of Thy glory." We had to ascend to heaven in Christ to see and to understand the creation in its real being as glorification of God, as that *response* to divine love in which alone creation becomes what God wants it to be: thanksgiving, eucharist, adoration. It is here—in the heavenly dimension of the Church, with "thousands of Archangels and myriads of Angels, with the Cherubim and Seraphim . . . who soar aloft, borne on their pinions . . ."—that we can finally "express ourself," and this expression is:

> Holy, Holy, Holy,
> Lord of Sabaoth.
> Heaven and earth are full of Thy glory.
> Hosanna in the highest.
> Blessed is He that cometh in the Name of the Lord.

This is the ultimate purpose of all that exists, the *end*, the goal and the fulfillment, because this is the *beginning*, the principle of Creation.

12

But as we stand before God, remembering all that He has done for us, and offer to Him our thanksgiving for all His benefits, we inescapably discover that the content of all this thanksgiving and remembrance is Christ. All remembrance is ultimately the remembrance of Christ, all thanksgiving is finally thanksgiving for Christ. "In Him was life and that life was the light of men." And in the light of the Eucharist we *see* that Christ is indeed the life and light of all that exists, and the glory that fills heaven and earth. There is nothing else to remember, nothing else to be thankful for, because in Him everything finds its being, its life, its end.

And the Sanctus, therefore, brings us so simply, so logically to that one man, one night, one event in which this world found once for all its judgment and its salvation. It is not that having sung the Sanctus and confessed the majesty of divine glory, we put this aside and go into the next subdivision of the prayer, the Remembrance. No, the Remembrance is the fullness of our doxology, it is again the eucharist that "naturally" leads us into the very heart and content of all remembrance and thanksgiving.

> Holy and most holy art Thou in Thy glorious majesty,
> Who hast so loved the world
> That Thou gavest Thine only-begotten Son,

That whosoever believeth on Him
Should not perish but have everlasting life,
Who, when He had come
And had performed all that was appointed for our sakes,
In the night on which he was given up, or
In which, rather, He did give Himself
For the life of the world,
Took bread in His holy and pure and sinless hands
And when He had given thanks, and blessed it, and sanctified it,
He gave it to His holy disciples, saying:
Take, eat, this is my Body which is broken for you
For the remission of sins.
And in like manner, after supper
He took the cup, saying:
Drink ye all of this: this is my Blood of the New Testament,
Which is shed for you, and for many
For the remission of sins.

As we stand before God, there is nothing else we can remember and bring with us and offer to God but this self-offering of Christ, because in it all thanksgiving, all remembrance, all offering—that is, the whole life of man and of the world—were fulfilled. And so:

Remembering this commandment of salvation,
And all those things which for our sakes were brought to pass,
The Cross,the Grave, the Resurrection on the third day,
The Ascension into Heaven, the Sitting on the right hand,
The Second and glorious Advent—
Thine own of thine own we offer unto Thee,
In behalf of all and for all. . . .

13

Up to this point the Eucharist was our ascension in Christ, our entrance in Him into the "world to come." And now, in this eucharistic offering in Christ of all things to the One to whom they belong and in whom alone they really exist, this movement of ascension has reached its *end.* We are at the paschal table of the Kingdom. What we have offered—our food, our life, ourselves, and the whole world—we offered in Christ and as Christ because He Himself has assumed our life and is our life. And now all this is given back to us as the gift of new life, and therefore—necessarily —as *food.*

"This is my body, this is my blood. Take, eat, drink. . . ." And generations upon generations of theologians ask the same questions. How is this possible? How does this happen? And what exactly does happen in this transformation? And when exactly? And what is the cause? No answer seems to be satisfactory. Symbol? But what is a symbol? Substance, accidents? Yet one immediately feels that something is lacking in all these theories, in which the Sacrament is reduced to the categories of time, substance, and causality, the very categories of "this world."

Something is lacking because the theologian thinks of the sacrament and forgets the liturgy. As a good scientist he first isolates the object of his study, reduces it to one moment, to one "phenomenon"—and then, proceeding from the general to the particular, from the known to the unknown, he gives a definition, which in fact raises more questions than it answers. But throughout our study the main point has been that the whole liturgy is *sacramental*, that is, one transforming act and one ascending movement. And the very goal of this movement of ascension is to take us out of "this world" and to make us partakers of the *world to come.* In *this world*—the one that condemned Christ and by doing so has condemned itself—no bread, no wine can become the body and blood of Christ. Nothing which is a *part* of it can be "sacralized." But the liturgy of the Church is always an *anaphora,* a lifting up, an ascension. The Church fulfills itself in heaven in that *new eon* which Christ has inaugurated in His death, resurrection and ascension, and which was given to the Church on the day of Pentecost as its life, as the "end" toward which it moves. In this world Christ is crucified, His body broken, and His blood shed. And we must go out of this world, we must ascend to heaven in Christ in order to become partakers of the world to come.

But this is not an "other" world, different from the one God has created and given to us. It is our same world, *already* perfected in Christ, but *not yet* in us. It is our same world, redeemed and restored, in which Christ "fills all things with Himself." And since God has created the world

as food for us and has given us food as means of communion with Him, of life in Him, the new food of the new
life which we receive from God in His Kingdom *is Christ
Himself*. He is our bread—because from the very beginning
all our hunger was a hunger for Him and all our bread was
but a symbol of Him, a symbol that had to become reality.

He became man and lived in this world. He ate and
drank, and this means that the world of which he partook,
the very food of our world became His body, His life. But
His life was totally, absolutely *eucharistic*—all of it was
transformed into communion with God and all of it ascended
into heaven. And now He shares this glorified life with us.
"What I have done alone—I give it now to you: take,
eat. . . ."

We offered the bread in remembrance of Christ because
we know that Christ is Life, and all food, therefore, must
lead us to Him. And now when we receive this bread from
His hands, we know that he has taken up all life, filled it
with Himself, made it what it was meant to be: communion
with God, sacrament of His presence and love. Only in
the Kingdom can we confess with St. Basil that "this bread is
in very truth the precious body of our Lord, this wine the
precious blood of Christ." What is "supernatural" here, in
this world, is revealed as "natural" there. And it is always in
order to lead us "there" and to make us what we are that
the Church fulfills herself in liturgy.

14

It is the Holy Spirit who *manifests* the bread as the body
and the wine as the blood of Christ.[1] The Orthodox
Church has always insisted that the *transformation (metab-
ole)* of the eucharistic elements is performed by the
epiclesis—the invocation of the Holy Spirit—and not by

---

[1]See the Liturgy of St. Basil: ". . . and manifest this bread as in very
truth the precious Body . . . this chalice as in very truth the precious
Blood. . ."

the words of institution. This doctrine, however, was often misunderstood by the Orthodox themselves. Its point is not to replace one "causality"—the words of institution—by another, a different "formula." It is to reveal the eschatological character of the sacrament. The Holy Spirit comes on the "last and great day" of Pentecost. He manifests the world to come. He inaugurates the Kingdom. He always takes us *beyond*. To be in the Spirit means to be in heaven, for the Kingdom of God is "joy and peace in the Holy Spirit." And thus in the Eucharist it is He who *seals* and *confirms* our ascension into heaven, who transforms the Church into the body of Christ and—therefore—*manifests* the elements of our offering as *communion in the Holy Spirit*. This is the consecration.

15

But before we can partake of the heavenly food there remains one last, absolutely essential act: the *intercession*. To be in Christ means to be like Him, to make ours the very movement of His life. And as He "ever liveth to make intercession" for all "that come unto God by him" (Heb 7:25), so we cannot help accepting His intercession as our own. The Church is not a society for escape—corporately or individually—from this world to taste of the mystical bliss of eternity. Communion is not a "mystical experience": we drink of the chalice of Christ, and He gave Himself for the life of the world. The bread on the paten and the wine in the chalice are to remind us of the incarnation of the Son of God, of the cross and death. And thus it is the very joy of the Kingdom that makes us *remember* the world and pray for it. It is the very communion with the Holy Spirit that enables us to love the world with the love of Christ. The Eucharist is the sacrament of unity and the *moment of truth*: here we see the world in Christ, as it really is, and not from our particular and therefore limited and partial points of view. Intercession begins here, in the glory of the messianic banquet, and this is the only true beginning for the

Church's mission. It is when, "having put aside all earthly care," we seem to have left *this world,* that we, in fact, recover it in all its reality.

Intercession constitutes, thus, the only real preparation for communion. For in and through communion not only do we become one body and one spirit, but we are restored to that solidarity and love which the world has lost. And the great Eucharistic Prayer is now summed up in the Lord's Prayer, each petition of which implies the total and complete dedication to God's Kingdom in the world. It is *His* prayer, and He *gave* it to us, made it our prayer, as He made his Father *our* Father. No one has been "worthy" to receive communion, no one has been *prepared* for it. At this point all merits, all righteousness, all devotions disappear and dissolve. Life comes again to us as *Gift,* a free and divine gift. This is why in the Orthodox Church we call the eucharistic elements Holy Gifts. Adam is again introduced into Paradise, taken out of nothingness and crowned king of creation. Everything is free, nothing is due and yet all is given. And, therefore, the greatest humility and obedience is to *accept* the gift, to say yes—in joy and gratitude. There is nothing we can *do,* yet we become all that God wanted us to be from eternity, when we are *eucharistic.*

16

And now the time has come for us to *return into the world.* "Let us depart in peace," says the celebrant as he leaves the altar, and this is the last *commandment* of the liturgy. We must not stay on Mount Tabor, although we know that it is good for us to be there. We are sent back. But now "we have seen the true Light, we have received the heavenly Spirit." And it is as witnesses of this Light, as witnesses of the Spirit, that we must "go forth" and begin the never-ending mission of the Church. Eucharist was the *end* of the journey, the end of time. And now it is again the *beginning,* and things that were impossible are again revealed to us as possible. The time of the world has become the time of the Church, the time of salvation and redemption. And God has made us *competent,* as Paul Claudel has said, competent to be His witnesses, to fulfill what He has done and is ever doing. This is the meaning of the Eucharist; this is why the mission of the Church begins in the liturgy of ascension, for it alone makes possible the liturgy of mission.

3

The Time of Mission

As we leave the church after the Sunday Eucharist we enter again into time, and time, therefore, is the first "object" of our Christian faith and action. For it is indeed the icon of our fundamental reality, of the optimism as well as of the pessimism of our life, of life as life and of life as death. Through time on the one hand we experience life as a possibility, growth, fulfillment, as a movement toward a future. Through time, on the other hand, all future is dissolved in death and annihilation. Time is the only reality of life, yet it is a strangely nonexistent reality: it constantly dissolves life in a past which no longer is, and in a future which always leads to death. By itself time is nothing but a line of telegraph poles strung out into the distance and at some point along the way is our death.

All generations, all philosophers have always been aware of this anxiety of time, of its paradox. All philosophy, all religion is ultimately an attempt to solve the "problem of time." And thousands of books, Christian and non-Christian, have been written about it. It is not our purpose, however, to add another "theology of time" to all those that exist already. It is rather to describe very briefly the experience of time which Christians have had from the very beginning and which is still given to them in the Church. Here again what the Church offers is not a "solution" of a philosophical problem, but a *gift*. And it becomes solution only as it is accepted as freely and joyfully as it is given.

Or, it may be, the joy of that gift makes both the problem
and the solution unnecessary, irrelevant.

2

To understand the gift we shall once more turn to the
liturgy, decipher again its forgotten language. Today no
one, except the peculiar and esoteric race of men called
"liturgiologists," is interested in what was in the past a
major preoccupation for Christians: the feasts and the
seasons, the cycles of prayer, a very real concern about the
"kairos"—the time of liturgical celebration. Not only the
average layman, even the theologian seems to say: the world
of Christian "symbolism" is no longer our world, all this
failed, all this is gone and we have more serious affairs to
attend to; it would be unthinkable, ridiculous to try to
solve any real "problem" of modern life by referring it, say,
to Easter or Pentecost, or even to Sunday.

Yet at this point let us ask a few questions. Are these
"symbols" merely "symbolic"? Or is their failure perhaps to
be explained precisely by the symbolic value attached to
them by Christians themselves, who ceased to understand
their true nature? And did they not cease to understand
this nature because at one time (it would take too long to
elaborate on this here) Christians came to think that "religion" has nothing to do with time, is in fact salvation from
time? Before we gain the right to dispose of the old "symbols" we must understand that the real tragedy of Christianity is not its "compromise" with the world and progressive "materialism," but on the contrary, its "spiritualization"
and transformation into "religion." And religion—as we
know already—has thus come to mean a world of pure
spirituality, a concentration of attention on matters per-
taining to the "soul." Christians were tempted to reject
time altogether and replace it with mysticism and "spiritual" pursuits, to live as Christians out of time and thereby
escape its frustrations; to insist that time has no real meaning from the point of view of the Kingdom which is "beyond

time." And they finally succeeded. They left time meaningless indeed, although full of Christian "symbols." And
today they themselves do not know what to do with these
symbols. For it is impossible to "put Christ back into
Christmas" if He has not redeemed—that is, made meaningful—time itself.

We must understand, therefore, that the intensive, almost pathological, preoccupation of our modern world with
time and its "problem" is rooted in this specifically Christian failure. It is because of us, Christians, that the world in
which we live has literally *no time.* Is it not true that the
more "time-saving" devices we invent, the less time we
have? The joyless *rush* is interrupted by *relaxation* ("sit
back and relax!"), but such is the horror of the strange
vacuum covered by this truly demonic word, "relaxation,"
that men must take pills to endure it, and buy expensive
books about how to *kill* this no man's land of "modern
living."

There is *no time* because Christianity, on the one hand,
made it impossible for man to live in the old natural time,
broke beyond repair the cycle of the eternal return. It has
announced the fullness of time, revealed time as history
and fulfillment, and has truly poisoned us once for all with
the dream of a meaningful time. There is no time, on the
other hand, because having announced all this, Christianity
abandoned time, invited Christians simply to leave it and
to think of eternity as of an eternal rest (if not yet "relaxation"). To be sure, one can still adorn the meaningless
time with "beautiful symbols" and "colorful rites," preferably
"ancient." One can—at regular intervals and by consulting
the "rubrics"—change the colors of liturgical vestments,
and spice the same eternal sermon with some references to
Easter, or Christmas, or Epiphany. All this, "inspiring" and
"uplifting" as it may be, has no meaning for the real time
in which the real man must live, or rather, for the absence
of time, which makes his life a nightmarish alternation of
"rush" and "relaxation."

And thus our question is: did Christ, the Son of God,
rise from the dead on the *first day* of the week, did He send

His Spirit on the day of *Pentecost,* did He, in other words,
enter time only that we may "symbolize" it in fine celebrations which, although connected with the days and the
hours, have no power to give time a real meaning, to transform and redeem it?

3

From the beginning Christians had their own *day,* and it is
in its peculiar nature that we find the key to the Christian
experience of time. To recover it, however, we must go
beyond Constantine's legislation which, by instituting Sunday as the compulsory, weekly day of rest, made it the
Christian substitute for the Jewish Sabbath. After that the
unique and paradoxical significance of the Lord's Day was
little by little forgotten. And yet its significance came precisely from its relation to the Sabbath, that is, to the whole
biblical understanding of time. In the Jewish religious
experience Sabbath, the seventh day, has a tremendous
importance: it is the participation by man in, and his affirmation of, the *goodness* of God's creation. "And God saw it
was good. . . . And God blessed the seventh day, and
sanctified it: because in it he had rested from all his work
which God created and made" (Gn. 1:25, 2:3). The seventh
day is thus the joyful acceptance of the world created by God
as *good.* The rest prescribed on that day, and which was
somehow obscured later by petty and legalistic prescriptions
and taboos, is not at all our modern "relaxation," an *absence*
of work. It is the active participation in the "Sabbath delight,"
in the sacredness and fullness of divine peace as the fruit
of all work, as the crowning of all time. It has thus both
cosmic and eschatological connotations.

Yet this "good" world, which the Jew blesses on the
seventh day, is at the same time the world of sin and revolt
against God, and its time is the time of man's exile and
alienation from God. And, therefore, the seventh day points
beyond itself toward a new Lord's Day—the day of salvation and redemption, of God's triumph over His enemies.

In the late Jewish apocalyptic writings there emerges the idea of a new day which is both the *eighth*—because it is beyond the frustrations and limitations of "seven," the time of *this world*—and the *first*, because with it begins the new time, that of the Kingdom. It is from this idea that grew the Christian Sunday.

Christ rose from the dead on the *first day* after Sabbath. The life that shone forth from the grave was beyond the inescapable limitations of "seven," of time that leads to death. It was thus the beginning of a new life and of a new time. It was truly the eighth and the first day and it became the day of the Church. The risen Christ, according to the fourth Gospel, appeared to His disciples on the first day (Jn. 20:19) and then "after eight days" (20:26). This is the day on which the Church celebrates the Eucharist—the sacrament of its ascension to the Kingdom and of its participation at the messianic banquet in the "age to come," the day on which the Church fulfills itself as new life. The earliest documents mention that Christians meet *statu die*— on a fixed day—and nothing in the long history of Christianity could alter the importance of this fixed day.

A "fixed day." . . . If Christianity were a purely "spiritual" and eschatological faith there would have been no need for a "fixed day," because mysticism has no interest in time. To save one's soul one needs, indeed, no "calendar." And if Christianity were but a new "religion," it would have established its calendar, with the usual opposition between the "holy days" and the "profane days"—those to be "kept" and "observed" and those religiously insignificant. Both understandings did in fact appear later. But this was not at all the original meaning of the "fixed day." It was not meant to be a "holy day" opposed to profane ones, a commemoration in time of a past event. Its true meaning was in the transformation of time, not of calendar. For, on the one hand, Sunday remained *one of the days* (for more than three centuries it was not even a day of rest), the first of the week, fully belonging to *this* world. Yet on the other hand, on that day, through the eucharistic ascension, the Day of the Lord was revealed and manifested in all its glory and transforming power as the *end* of this world, as the *beginning* of the world to come. And thus through that one day all days, all time were transformed into times of *remembrance and expectation,* remembrance of this ascension, ("we have seen the true light") and expectation of its *coming.* All days, all hours were now referred to this *end* of all "natural" life, to the *beginning* of the new life. The week was no longer a sequence of "profane" days, with rest on the "sacred" day at their end. It was now a movement from Mount Tabor into the world, from the world into the "day without evening" of the world to come. Every day, every hour acquired now an importance, a gravity it could not have had before: each day was now to be a *step* in this movement, a moment of decision and witness, a time of ultimate meaning. Sunday therefore was not a "sacred" day to be "observed" apart from all other days and opposed to them. It did not interrupt time with a "timeless" mystical ecstasy. It was not a "break" in an otherwise meaningless sequence of days and nights. By remaining one of the ordinary days, and yet by revealing itself through the Eucharist as the eighth and first day, it gave all days their true meaning. It made the time of this world a time of the *end,* and it made it also the time of the *beginning.*

4

We must turn now to the second dimension of the Christian experience of time—to the so-called "Christian year." To speak of it, however, is even more difficult than to speak of Sunday, because for the modern Christian the relation between this "Christian year" and time has become incomprehensible and, therefore, irrelevant. On certain dates the Church commemorates certain events of the past —nativity, resurrection, the descent of the Holy Spirit. These dates are an occasion for a liturgical "illustration" of certain theological affirmations, but as such they are in no way related to the real time or of consequence to it. Even within the Church itself they are mere "breaks" in the normal routine of its activities, and many business minded and action-oriented Christians secretly consider these festivals and celebrations a waste of time. And if other Christians welcome them as additional days of rest and "vacation," no one seriously thinks of them as the very heart of the Church's life and mission. There exists, in other words, a serious crisis in the very idea of a feast, and it is here that we must begin our brief discussion of the Christian year.

Feast means *joy.* Yet, if there is something that we—the serious, adult and frustrated Christians of the twentieth century—look at with suspicion, it is certainly joy. How can one be joyful when so many people suffer? When so many things are to be done? How can one indulge in festivals and celebrations when people expect from us "serious" answers to their problems? Consciously or subconsciously Christians have accepted the whole ethos of our joyless and business-minded culture. They believe that the only way to be taken "seriously" by the "serious"—that is, by modern man—is to be serious, and, therefore, to reduce to a symbolic "minimum" what in the past was so tremendously central in the life of the Church—the joy of a feast. The modern world has relegated joy to the category of "fun" and "relaxation." It is justified and permissible on our "time off"; it is a concession, a compromise. And Christians have come to believe all this, or rather they have ceased to believe that the feast, the joy have something to do precisely with the "serious problems" of life itself, may even be *the* Christian answer to them. With all these spiritual and cultural connotations, the "Christian year"—the sequence of liturgical commemorations and celebrations—ceased to be the generator of power, and is now looked upon as a more or less antiquated decoration of religion. It is used as a kind of "audio-visual" aid in religious education, but it is neither a root of Christian life and action, nor a "goal" toward which they are oriented.

To understand the true nature—and "function"—of feasts we must remember that Christianity was born and preached at first in cultures in which feasts and celebrations were an organic and essential part of the whole world view and way of life. For the man of the past a feast was not something accidental and "additional": it was his way of putting *meaning* into his life, of liberating it from the animal rhythm of work and rest. A feast was not a simple "break" in the otherwise meaningless and hard life of work, but a justification of that work, its fruit, its—so to speak— sacramental transformation into joy and, therefore, into freedom. A feast was thus always deeply and organically related to time, to the natural cycles of time, to the whole framework of man's life in the world. And, whether we want it or not, whether we like it or not, Christianity *accepted* and made its own this fundamentally human phenomenon of feast, as it accepted and made its own the whole man and all his needs. But, as in everything else, Christians accepted the feast not only by giving it a new meaning, by transforming its "content," but by taking it, along with the whole of "natural" man, through death and resurrection.

Yes, as we have already said, Christianity was on the one hand the end of all natural joy. It revealed its impossibility, its futility, its sadness—because by revealing the perfect man it revealed the abyss of man's alienation from God and the inexhaustible sadness of this alienation. The cross of Christ signified an end of all "natural" rejoicing; it made it, indeed, impossible. From this point of view the sad "seriousness" of modern man is certainly of Christian origin, even if this has been forgotten by that man himself. Since the Gospel was preached in this world, all attempts to go back to a pure "pagan joy," all "renaissances," all "healthy optimisms" were bound to fail. "There is but one sadness," said Leon Bloy, "that of not being a saint." And it is this sadness that permeates mysteriously the whole life of the world, its frantic and pathetic hunger and thirst for perfection, which kills all joy. Christianity made it impossible simply to rejoice in the natural cycles—in harvests and new moons. Because it relegated the perfection of joy to the inaccessible future—as the goal and end of all work—it made all human life an "effort," a "work."

Yet, on the other hand Christianity was the revelation and the gift of joy, and thus, the gift of genuine *feast*. Every Saturday night at the resurrection vigil we sing, "for, through the Cross, joy came into the whole world." This joy is pure joy because it does not depend on anything in this world, and is not the reward of anything in us. It is totally and absolutely a *gift*, the *"charis,"* the grace. And being pure gift, this joy has a transforming power, *the only really transforming power in this world*. It is the "seal" of the Holy Spirit on the life of the Church—on its faith, hope and love.

5

"Through the Cross joy came *into the whole world"*—and not just to some men as their personal and private joy. Once more, were Christianity pure "mysticism," pure "eschatology," there would be no need for feasts and celebrations. A holy soul would keep its secret feast apart from the world, to the extent that it could free itself from its time. But joy was given to the Church *for the world*—that the Church might be a witness to it and transform the world by joy. Such is the "function" of Christian feasts and the meaning of their belonging to time.

For us today Easter and Pentecost—to limit ourselves to the two initial and fundamental feasts which give true significance to the Christian year—are primarily the annual commemorations of two events of the past: Christ's resurrection and the descent of the Holy Spirit. But what is "commemoration"? Is not the whole life of the Church a constant remembrance of the death and resurrection of Christ? Is not its whole life called to be the manifestation of the Holy Spirit? In the Orthodox Church, each Sunday is the day of resurrection and each Eucharist a Pentecost. In fact, the understanding of feasts as *historical* commemorations which emerged little by little after Constantine meant a transformation of their initial meaning and, strange as it may seem, divorced them from their living connection with real time. Thus in Australia today Easter is celebrated in the fall and no one seems to find it odd, because for several centuries the Christian calendar was understood as a system of *holy days* to be observed within time, that is, among "profane" days, but without any special relation to them.

But if the early Church adopted or, rather, simply kept as its own, the great Jewish festivals of Passover and Pentecost, it was not because they reminded it of Christ's resurrection and the coming of the Spirit (its remembrance was the very essence of the Church's whole life), but because they were, even before Christ, the announcement, the anticipation of that experience of time and of life in time, of which the Church was the manifestation and the fulfillment. They were—to use another image—the "material" of a *sacrament of time* to be performed by the Church. We know that both feasts originated as the annual celebration of spring and of the first fruits of nature. In this respect they were the very expression of feast as man's *joy about life*. They celebrated the world coming back to life again after the death of winter, becoming again the food and life of man. And it is very significant that this most "natural," all-embracing and universal feast—that of life itself—became the starting point, and indeed the foundation of the long transformation of the idea and experience of feast. It is equally significant that in this transformation each new stage did not abolish and simply replace the previous one, but fulfilled it in an even deeper and greater meaning until the whole process was consummated in Christ Himself. The mystery of *natural* time, the bondage to winter and release in spring, was fulfilled in the mystery of time as *history*— the bondage to Egypt and the release into the Promised Land. And the mystery of historical time was transformed into the mystery of eschatological time, of its understanding as *passover*—the "passage" into the ultimate joy of salvation and redemption, as movement toward the fulfillment of the Kingdom. And when Christ "our Passover" (1 Cor 5:7), performed His *passage* to the Father, He assumed and fulfilled all these meanings—the whole movement of time in all its dimensions; and on the "last and great day of Pentecost" He inaugurated the new time, the new "eon" of the Spirit.

And thus Easter is not a commemoration of an event, but—every year—the fulfillment of time itself, of our real time. For we still live in the same three dimensions of time: in the world of nature, in the world of history, in the world of expectation. And in each one of them man is in a secret search for joy, that is, for an ultimate meaning and perfection, for an ultimate fulfillment which he does not find. Time always points to a feast, to a joy, which by itself it cannot give or realize. So needful of *meaning,* time becomes the very form and image of *meaninglessness.*

But on Easter night the meaning is given. And it is not given by means of "explanation" or even "commemoration," but as a gift of joy itself, the joy of participation in the new time of the Kingdom. To experience this, one has to go to an Orthodox Church on Easter night, after the procession has gone around the church and has stopped in the darkness at the closed door. And now the doors are opened with the announcement: "Christ is risen!" The Paschal celebration has begun. What is this night of which St. Gregory of Nyssa says that it becomes brighter than the day and which the Orthodox call the "bright night"? One could describe the various rites, one could analyze the texts, one could mention a thousand details, but in the last count, all this is secondary. The only reality is joy and this joy is *given.*

> Enter ye all into the joy of your Lord,
> You who are rich and you the poor, come to the feast,
> Receive all the riches of loving-kindness . . .
> And let no one bewail his poverty,
> *For the universal Kingdom has been revealed.*

And the whole service is nothing but a response to this joy, its acceptance, its celebration, the affirmation of its reality.

> The *Pascha* (passover) of the Lord.
> From death unto life,

And from earth unto heaven
Has Christ our God brought us . . . .

Now are all things filled with light,
Heaven and earth and the places under the earth.
All Creation does celebrate the Resurrection of Christ
On whom it is founded . . . .

We celebrate the death of Death,
The annihilation of Hell,
The beginning of a life new and everlasting.
And with ectasy we sing praises to the author thereof . . . .

This is the chosen and holy Day,
The one King and Lord of Sabbaths,
The Feast of Feasts and the Triumph of Triumphs . . . .

O Christ, the Passover great and most holy!
O Wisdom, Word and Power of God!
Grant that we may more perfectly partake of Thee
In the day of Thy Kingdom which knoweth no night.

We called Easter the "sacrament of time." Indeed, the *joy* given on that night, the light that transforms the night into a night "brighter than day" is to become the secret joy and the ultimate meaning of all time, and thus *transform* the year into a "Christian year." After the Easter night comes the morning, and then another night and another new day. Time begins again, but it is now filled from "inside" with that unique and truly "eschatological" experience of joy. A ray of sun on a gloomy factory wall, the smile on a human face, each rainy morning, the fatigue of each evening—all is now referred to this joy and not only points beyond itself, but can also be a sign, a mark, a secret "presence" of that joy.

For fifty days after Easter it is granted to us to live in the paschal joy, to experience time as the *feast.* And then comes the "last and great" day of Pentecost and with it our return into the real time of this world. At Vespers of that day the Christians are told—for the first time since Easter—to kneel. The night is approaching, the night of time and history, of the daily effort, of the fatigue and temptations, of the whole inescapable burden of life. The Easter season is at its end—but as we enter the night, we know that the end has been transformed into a beginning, that all time is now the time *after Pentecost* (that is why we number all Sundays from this point until the next Easter season). This is the time in which the joy of the Kingdom, the "peace and joy" of the Holy Spirit, is at work. "There shall be no separation, O friends! said Christ. . . ."

Time itself is now measured by the rhythm of the end and the beginning, of the end transformed into beginning, of the beginning announcing the fulfillment. The Church is *in time* and its life in this world is *fasting,* that is, a life of effort, sacrifice, self-denial and dying. The Church's very mission is to become all things to all men. But how could the Church fulfill this mission, how could it be the salvation of the world, if it were not, first of all and above everything else, the divine gift of Joy, the fragrance of the Holy Spirit, the presence here in time of the feast of the Kingdom?

6

After the week and the year—the day: the most direct and immediate unit of time. It is here, in the reality of daily life, that the theology of time, expressed in the experience of Sunday and Easter, must find its application. We realize, of course, that the daily cycle of services, abandoned long ago, is not very likely to be restored. Yet, what *is* to be restored, or rather, rediscovered, is the relation of the Church and of the individual Christian to the time of the day, the relation which was (and theoretically still is) the theme, the content of the daily services. For these were not meant to be "prayer breaks," periods of spiritual refreshment and "peace of mind," but truly *liturgical acts,* that is, acts performed on behalf of and for the whole community, as an essential part of the redeeming mission of the Church.

Contrary to our secular experience of time, the liturgical day begins with Vespers, i.e., in the evening. This is, of course, the reminiscence of the biblical "And the evening and the morning were the first day" (Gn. 1:5). Yet it is more than a reminiscence. For it is, indeed, the end of each "unit" of time that reveals its pattern and meaning, that gives to time its reality. Time is always growth, but only at the end can we discern the direction of that growth and see its fruits. It is at the end, in the evening of each day that God sees His creation as *good;* it is at the end of creation that He gives it to man. And thus, it is at the end of the day that the Church begins the liturgy of time's sanctification.

We come to church, we who are in the world having lived through many hours filled, as usual, with work and rest, suffering and joy, hatred and love. Men died and men were born. For some it was the happiest day of their life, a day to be remembered forever. And for some others it brought the end of all their hopes, the destruction of their very soul. And the whole day is now here—unique, irreversible, irreparable. It is gone, but its results, its fruits will shape the next day, for what we have done once remains forever.

But the vesperal service does not begin as a religious "epilogue" of the day, as a prayer *added* to all its other experience. It begins at the *beginning,* and this means in the "rediscovery," in adoration and thanksgiving, of the world as God's creation. The Church takes us, as it were, to that first evening on which man, called by God to life, opened his eyes and saw what God in His love was giving to him, saw all the beauty, all the glory of the temple in which he was standing, and rendered thanks to God. And in this thanksgiving he *became himself.*

> Praise the Lord, O my soul. Blessed art Thou O Lord . . . .
> O Lord, how manifold are thy works. In wisdom hast Thou
>   made them all.
> The earth is full of Thy riches.
> I will sing unto the Lord as long as I live,
> I will praise my God, while I have my being (Ps. 104).

And it must be so. There must be someone in this world —which rejected God and in this rejection, in this blasphemy, became a chaos of darkness—there must be someone to stand in its center, and to discern, to see it again as full of divine riches, as the cup full of life and joy, as

beauty and wisdom, and to thank God for it. This "someone" is Christ, the new Adam who restores that "eucharistic life" which I, the old Adam, have rejected and lost; who
makes me again what I am, and restores the world to me.
And if the Church *is in Christ,* its initial act is always this
act of thanksgiving, of returning the world to God.

Through contrast with the beauty and wonder of creation,
however, the darkness and failure of the world is discovered,
and this is the second great theme of Vespers. If Psalm 104
speaks truly, the world as we know it is—by contrast—a
nightmare. Because we have first seen the beauty of the
world, we can now see the ugliness, realize what we have
lost, understand how our whole life (and not only some
"trespasses") has become sin, and can *repent* it. The lights
are now extinguished. The "royal doors" of the sanctuary
are closed. The celebrant has put off his vestments; it is
the naked and suffering man who cries outside of Paradise, who in full awareness of his exile, of his betrayal, of
his darkness, says to God: "Out of the deep have I cried
unto Thee, O Lord." In the face of the glory of creation
there must be a tremendous sadness. God has given us another day, and we can see just how we have destroyed this
gift of His. We are not "nice" Christians come apart from
the ugly world. If we do not stand precisely as representa-
tives of this world, as indeed the world itself, if we do not
bear the whole burden of *this* day, our "piety" may still be
pious, but it is not Christian.

Now comes the third theme of Vespers: *redemption.*
Into this world of sin and darkness light has come: "O
gladsome radiance of the holy glory of the Father, immortal,
heavenly, holy, blessed, Jesus Christ." The world is at its
evening because the One bringing the final meaning to the
world has come; in the darkness of this world, the light of
Christ reveals again the true nature of things. This is not
the world it was before Christ came: His coming now *belongs* to the world. The decisive event of the cosmos has
taken place. We know now that the event of Christ must
transform everything to do with our lives. It was only because of Christ that we had the heart to glory in the crea-

tion at the beginning of Vespers, only because He gave us the eyes to "behold God's gracious hand in all his works." Now in the time in which we can thank God for Christ, we begin to understand that everything is transformed in Christ into its true wonder. In the radiance of His light the world is not commonplace. The very floor we stand on is a miracle of atoms whizzing about in space. The darkness of sin is clarified, and its burden shouldered. Death is robbed of its finality, trampled down by Christ's death. In a world where everything that seems to be present is immediately past, everything in Christ is able to participate in the eternal present of God. This very evening is the real time of our life.

And thus we are brought to the last theme of Vespers: that of the *end*. It is announced by the singing of the *Nunc Dimittis*. The words are attributed in the Gospel to the old man Simeon, who had spent his life in constant expectation of the coming Messiah because he had been told in a vision that he would not die before he saw the promised one of Israel. When Mary and Joseph brought the child Jesus to be presented to God in the temple, he was there and received Him into his arms, and the Gospel records that he said:

> Lord, now lettest Thou Thy servant depart in peace, according to Thy word. For mine eyes have seen Thy Salvation, which Thou hast prepared before the face of all people; to be a light to lighten the Gentiles, and to be the glory of thy people Israel.

Simeon had been waiting all his life, and then at last the Christ Child was given to him: he held the Life of the world in his arms. He stood for the whole world in its expectation and longing, and the words he used to express his thanksgiving have become our own. He could recognize the Lord because he had expected Him; he took Him into his arms because it is natural to take someone you love into your arms; and then his life of waiting was fulfilled. He had beheld the One he had longed for. He had completed his purpose in life, and he was ready to die.

But death to him was no catastrophe. It was only a natural expression of the fulfillment of his waiting. He was not closing his eyes to the light he had at last seen; his death was only the beginning of a more inward vision of that light. In the same way Vespers is the recognition that the evening of this world has come which announces the day that has no evening. In this world every day faces night; the world itself is facing night. It cannot last forever. Yet the Church is affirming that an evening is not only an end, but also a beginning, just as any evening is also the beginning of another day. In Christ and through Christ it may become the beginning of a *new life,* of the day that has no evening. For our eyes have seen salvation and a light which will never fail. And because of this, the time of this world is now pregnant with new life. We come into the presence of Christ to offer Him our time, we extend our arms to receive Him. And He fills this time with Himself, He heals it and makes it—again and again—the time of salvation.

7

"And the evening and the morning. . . ." When we first wake up, the initial sensation is always that of night, not of illumination; we are at our weakest, at our most helpless. It is like a man's first real experience of life in all its absurdity and solitude, at first kept from him by family warmth. We discover every morning in the amorphous darkness the inertia of life. And thus the first theme of Matins is again the coming of light into darkness. It begins not like Vespers with the creation, but with the Fall. Yet in this very helplessness and despair, there is a hidden expectation, a thirst and hunger. And within this scene the Church declares her joy, not only against the grain of natural life, but fulfilling it. The Church announces every morning that God is the Lord, and she begins to organize life around God.

In the church the first lights of Matins are candles, as a foretaste of the sun. Then the sun itself rises, dispelling the darkness of the world, and in this the Church sees the rising of the true Light of the world, the Son of God. We know that our Redeemer lives, and that in the midst of the ab-

surdity of life, He will be again revealed to us. Though the
misfortunes of life "compass us about," yet each morning
we can proclaim with the rising sun the coming of the long-
expected Messiah. Despite everything, "this is the day
which the Lord has made—we will rejoice and be glad in it.
Blessed is He that cometh in the Name of the Lord."

As the light grows, the service refers the new morning to
the new time. As Vespers referred evening to the whole
Christian experience of the world as "evening," so Matins
refers morning to the Christian experience of the Church
as "morning," as beginning.

These two complementary, yet absolutely essential, *dimensions* of time shape our life in time and, by giving time
a new meaning, transform it into *Christian time.* This
double experience is, indeed, to be applied to everything we
do. We are always *between* morning and evening, *between*
Sunday and Sunday, *between* Easter and Easter, *between*
the two comings of Christ. The experience of time as *end*
gives an absolute importance to whatever we do *now,*
makes it final, decisive. The experience of time as *beginning*
fills all our time with joy, for it adds to it the "coefficient"
of eternity: "I shall not die but live and declare the works
of the Lord." We are at work in the world, and this work
—in fact, any work—if analyzed in terms of the world in
itself, becomes meaningless, futile, irrelevant. In every city
in the world there is each morning a rush of clean and
shaven people getting to work. And every evening there is
a rush of the same people, now tired and dirty, going in the
opposite direction. But long, long ago a wise man looked at
this rush (its forms change, but not its meaninglessness)
and said:

> Vanity of vanities. All is vanity.
> What profit hath man of all his labor which he taketh under
>   the sun?
> One generation passeth away and another generation cometh;
> But the earth abideth forever.
> The eye is not satisfied with seeing, nor the ear filled with
>   hearing.
> There is no new thing under the sun. . . . (Eccl. 1)

And this remains true of the *fallen* world. But we Christians have too often forgotten that God has redeemed the world. For centuries we have preached to the hurrying people: your daily rush has no meaning, yet accept it—and you will be rewarded in *another* world by an eternal rest. But God revealed and offers us eternal Life and not eternal rest. And God revealed this eternal Life in the midst of time—and of its *rush*—as its secret meaning and goal. And thus he made time, and our work in it, into the *sacrament of the world to come,* the liturgy of fulfillment and ascension. It is when we have reached the very end of the world's self-sufficiency that it *begins* again for us as the material of the sacrament that we are to fulfill in Christ.

"There is no new thing under the sun." Yet every day, every minute resounds now with the victorious affirmation: "Behold, I make all things new. I am Alpha and Omega, the beginning and the end ..." (Rev. 21: 5—6).

4

Of Water and the Spirit

All that we have said about time and its transformation and renewal has simply no meaning if there is no new man to perform the sacrament of time. It is of him that we must speak now and of the act in which the newness of life and the power to live by it are given him. We began, however, not at baptism, which is the beginning of Christian life, but with the Eucharist and time, because it was essential to establish the cosmic dimensions of the life given in baptism. For a long time the theological and spiritual interest in baptism was virtually disconnected from its cosmic significance, from the totality of man's relation to the world. It was explained as man's liberation from "original sin." But both original sin and the liberation from it were given an extremely narrow and individual meaning. Baptism was understood as the means to assure the individual salvation of man's soul. No wonder that such an understanding of baptism led to a similar narrowing of the baptismal liturgy. From an act of the whole Church, involving the whole cosmos, it became a private ceremony, performed in a corner of the church by "private appointment," and in which the Church was reduced to the "minister of sacraments" and the cosmos to the three symbolic drops of water, considered as "necessary and sufficient" for the "validity" of the sacrament. *Validity* was the preoccupation—and not fullness, meaning, joy. Because of the obsession of baptismal theology with juridical and not ontological terms, the real question—*what* is made valid?—often remained unanswered.

Lately, it is true, there has occurred throughout the Christian world a certain widening of the theology of baptism. There has been a rediscovery of the meaning of baptism as entrance and integration into the Church, of its "ecclesiological" significance. But ecclesiology, unless it is given its true cosmic perspective ("for the life of the world"), unless it is understood as the Christian form of "cosmology," is always ecclesiolatry, the Church considered as a "being in itself" and not the new relation of God, man and the world. And it is not "ecclesiology" that gives baptism its true meaning; it is rather in and through baptism that we find the first and fundamental meaning of the Church.

Baptism, by its very form and elements—the water of the baptismal font, the oil of christmation—refers us inescapably to "matter," to the world, to the cosmos. In the early Church the celebration of baptism took place during the solemn Easter vigil, and in fact, the Easter liturgy grew out of the "Paschal mystery" of baptism. This means that baptism was understood as having a direct meaning for the "new time," of which Easter is the celebration and the manifestation. And finally, baptism and chrismation were always fulfilled in the Eucharist—which is the sacrament of the Church's ascension to the Kingdom, the sacrament of the "world to come."

I have already said that the tragedy of a certain theology (and piety) was that in its search for precise definitions, it artificially isolated the sacraments from the liturgy in which they were performed. The liturgy was relegated to the category of secondary, decorative and ritual elements having no bearing on the *"esse"* of the sacrament. By doing so, however, theology lost much of the true understanding of the sacramental reality. Baptism in particular has suffered an almost disastrous loss of meaning. And we must, therefore —in order to recover it—return to the *"leitourgia"* of the Church.

2

In the past, preparation for baptism sometimes lasted as long as three years. Now that infant baptism has become virtually universal however, this preparation is merely of historical interest. And yet it is important for us to remember that a great part of the Church's life was devoted to the preparation for baptism of the catechumens, those who already believed in Christ and were now on their way to the fulfillment of that faith in baptism. In the Orthodox Church, even today, the entire first part of the Eucharist is called the "Liturgy of the Catechumens." The liturgical seasons of Lent and Advent, the cycles of Christmas and Epiphany, the structure of Holy Week and, finally, the "solemnity of solemnities"—the Easter vigil—were all shaped in their development by the preparation for baptism and its celebration. The meaning of all this for us today is, first, that the whole life of the Church is, in a way, the explication and the manifestation of baptism, and second, that baptism forms the real content, the "existential" root of what we now call "religious education." The latter is not an abstract "knowledge about God" but the revelation of the wonderful things that have "happened" and happen to us in the divine gift of the new life.

The actual baptismal service as it is celebrated in the Orthodox Church begins with what was in the past the final act of the "catechumenate": the exorcisms, the renunciation of Satan and the confession of faith.

According to some modern interpreters of Christianity, "demonology" belongs to an antiquated world view and cannot be taken seriously by the man who "uses electricity." We cannot argue with them here. What we must affirm, what the Church has always affirmed, is that the use of electricity may be "demonic," as in fact may be the use of anything and of life itself. That is, in other words, the experience of evil which we call *demonic* is not that of a mere absence of good, or, for that matter, of all sorts of existential alienations and anxieties. It is indeed the *presence* of dark and irrational *power*. Hatred is not merely absence of love. It is certainly more than that, and we recognize its presence as an almost physical burden that we feel in our-selves when we hate. In our world in which normal and civilized men "used electricity" to exterminate six million human beings, in this world in which right now some ten million people are in concentration camps because they failed to understand the "only way to universal happiness," in this world the "demonic" reality is not a myth. And whatever the value or the consistency of its presentation in theologies and doctrines, it is this *reality* that the Church has in mind, that it indeed *faces* when at the moment of baptism, through the hands of the priest, it lays hold upon a new human being who has just entered life, and who, ac-cording to statistics, has a great likelihood some day of entering a mental institution, a penitentiary, or at best, the maddening boredom of a universal suburbia. The world from which the human being has received his life, and which will determine this life, is a prison. The Church did not have to wait for Kafka or Sartre to know it. But the Church also knows that the gates of this hell have been broken and that another Power has entered the world and claimed it for its true Owner. And that claim is not on souls alone, but on the totality of life, on the whole world. Thus —at the beginning of baptism—the Church makes that claim. The priest "breathes thrice in the face" of the cate-chumen, "and signeth his brow and his breast thrice with the sign of the cross and layeth his hand on the head saying:"

In Thy Name, O Lord God of Truth, and in the Name of Thine only-begotten Son, and of Thy Holy Spirit, I lay my hand upon Thy servant, who has been found worthy to flee unto Thy Holy Name, and to take refuge under the shelter of Thy wings. . . . Remove far from him his former delusion, and fill him with the faith, hope and love which are in Thee; that he may know that Thou art the only true God. . . . Enable him to walk in all Thy commandments and to fulfill those things which are well pleasing unto Thee, for if a man do those things, *he shall find life in them.* Make him to rejoice in the works of his hands, and in all his generation that he may render praise unto Thee, may sing, worship and glorify Thy great and exalted Name.

The exorcisms mean this: to face evil, to acknowledge its reality, to know its power, and to proclaim the power of

God to destroy it. The exorcisms announce the forthcoming baptism as an act of victory.

> Then the Priest turneth the person who is come to Baptism to the west, unclad, unshod, and having his hands uplifted, and he says,—
>
> "Dost thou renounce Satan, and all his Angels, and all his works, and all his services, and all his pride?"
>
> And the catechumen makes answer, or his sponsor for him, and says "I do."

The first act of the Christian life is a renunciation, a challenge. No one can be Christ's until he has, first, faced evil, and then become ready to *fight* it. How far is this spirit from the way in which we often proclaim, or to use a more modern term, "sell" Christianity today! Is it not usually presented as a comfort, help, release from tensions, a reasonable investment of time, energy and money? One has only to read—be it but once—the topics of the Sunday sermons announced in the Saturday newspapers, or the various syndicated "religious columns," to get the impression that "religion" is almost invariably presented as salvation from something—fear, frustration, anxiety—but never as the salvation of man and the world. How could we then speak of *"fight"* when the very set-up of our churches must, by definition, convey the idea of softness, comfort, peace? How can the Church use again the military language, which was its own in the first days, when it still thought of itself as *militia Christi?* One does not see very well where and how "fight" would fit into the weekly bulletin of a suburban parish, among all kinds of counseling sessions, bake sales, and "young adult" get-togethers.

And yet it is, indeed, the necessary condition of the next and decisive step.

"Dost thou unite thyself unto Christ?" says the priest, when he has turned—has *converted*—the catechumen to the east.

Then comes the *confession of faith,* the confession by the catechumen of the faith of the Church, of his acceptance of this faith and obedience to it. And again it is difficult to convince a modern Christian that to be the life of the world, the Church must not "keep smiling" at the world, putting the "All Welcome" signs on the churches, and adjusting its language to that of the last best seller. The beginning of the Christian life—of the life in the Church— is humility, obedience, and discipline. The last act of preparation for baptism, therefore, is this order:

> "Bow down also before Him." And the Catechumen answers, "I bow down before the Father, and the Son, and the Holy Spirit."

3

Baptism proper begins with the blessing of the water. To understand, however, the meaning of water here, one must stop thinking of it as an isolated "matter" of the sacrament. Or rather, one must realize that water is the "matter" of sacrament, because it stands for the whole of matter, which is, in baptism, the sign and presence of the world itself. In the biblical "mythological" world view—which incidentally is more meaningful and philosophically consistent than the one offered by some "demythologizers"—water is the *"prima materia,"* the basic element of the world. It is the natural symbol of life, for there is no life without water, but it is also the symbol of destruction and death, and finally, it is the symbol of purification, for there is no cleanliness without it. In the Book of Genesis creation of life is presented as the liberation of the dry land from the water— as a victory of the Spirit of God over the waters—the chaos of nonexistence. In a way, then, creation is a transformation of water into life.

What is important for us, however, is that the baptismal water represents the matter of the cosmos, the world as life of man. And its blessing at the beginning of the baptismal rite acquires thus a truly cosmic and redemptive significance. God created the world and blessed it and gave it to man as his food and life, as the means of communion with Him. The blessing of water signifies the return or redemption of matter to this initial and essential meaning. By accepting the baptism of John, Christ sanctified the water—made it the water of purification and reconciliation with God. It was then, as Christ was coming out of the water, that the Epiphany—the new and redemptive manifestation of God—took place, and the Spirit of God, who at the beginning of creation "moved upon the face of the waters," made water—that is, the world—again into what He made it at the beginning.

To bless, as we already know, is to give thanks. In and through thanksgiving, man acknowledges the true nature of things he receives from God, and thus makes them to be what they are. We bless and sanctify things when we offer them to God in a eucharistic movement of our whole being. And as we stand before the *water*—before the cosmos, the matter given to us by God—it is an all-embracing eucharistic movement which gives the baptismal liturgy its true beginning.

> Great art Thou, O Lord, and marvelous are Thy works, and there is no word which sufficeth to hymn Thy wonders. For Thou, of thine own good will, hast brought into being all things which before were not, and by Thy might Thou upholdest creation, and by Thy providence Thou orderest the world. . . .
> Before Thee tremble all the Powers endowed with intelligence. The Sun singeth unto Thee. The moon glorifieth Thee. The stars meet together before Thy presence. The light obeyeth Thee. The deeps tremble before Thee. . . .
> Thou didst come and didst save us!
> We confess Thy grace. We proclaim Thy mercy. We conceal not Thy gracious acts.

Once more the world is proclaimed to be what Christ revealed and made it to be—the gift of God to man, the means of man's communion with God. This water is manifested to us as "the grace of redemption," the remission of sins, the remedy of infirmities. "For we have called upon Thy Name, O Lord, and it is wonderful, and glorious, terrible to adversaries."

It is in this water that we now baptize—i.e., immerse—man, and this baptism is for him baptism *"into Christ"* (Rom. 6:3). For the faith in Christ that led this man to baptism is precisely the certitude that Christ is the only true "content"—meaning being and end—of all that exists,

the fullness of Him who fills all things. In faith the whole
world becomes the sacrament of His presence, the means of
life in Him. And water, the image and presence of the world,
is truly the image and presence of Christ.

But "know you not that so many of us as were baptized
into Jesus Christ, were baptized into his death?" (Rom.
6:3). Baptism—the gift of the "newness of life"—is announced as "the likeness of death." Why? Because the new
life which Christ gives to those who believe in Him shone
forth from the grave. This world rejected Christ, refused
to see in Him its own life and fulfillment. And since
it has no other life but Christ, by rejecting and killing
Christ the world condemned itself to death. Its only ultimate reality is death, and none of the secular eschatologies
in which men still put their hope can have any force against
the simple statement of Tolstoy: "And after a stupid life
there shall come a stupid death." But the Christian is precisely the one who knows that the true reality of the world
—of *this* world, of *this* life of ours—not of some mysterious
"other" world—is in Christ; the Christian knows, rather,
that Christ *is* this reality. In its self-sufficiency the world
and all that exists in it has no meaning. And as long as we
live after the fashion of this world, as long, in other words,
as we make our life an end in itself, no meaning and no
goal can stand, for they are dissolved in death. It is only when
we give up freely, totally, unconditionally, the self-sufficiency of our life, when we put all its meaning in Christ,
that the "newness of life"—which means a new possession
of the world—is given to us. The world then truly becomes
the sacrament of Christ's presence, the growth of the Kingdom and of life eternal. For Christ, "being raised from the
dead, dies no more; death has no more dominion over him."
Baptism is thus the death of our selfishness and self-sufficiency, and it is the "likeness of Christ's death" because
Christ's death is this unconditional self-surrender. And as
Christ's death "trampled down death" because in it the
ultimate meaning and strength of life were revealed, so also
does our dying with him unite us with the new "life in
God."

The meaning of this "newness of life" is manifested when the newly baptized person is clothed, immediately after baptism, in a *white garment*. It is the garment of a king. Man is again king of creation. The world is again his life, and not his death, for he knows what to do with it. He is restored to the joy and power of true human nature.

4

In the Orthodox Church, what we call today the second sacrament of initiation—that of chrismation (or confirmation)—has always been an integral part of the baptismal liturgy. For it is not so much another sacrament as the very fulfillment of baptism, its "confirmation" by the Holy Spirit. It can be distinguished from baptism only insofar as life can be distinguished from birth. The Holy Spirit *confirms* the whole life of the Church because He is that life, the manifestation of the Church as the "world to come," as the joy and peace of the Kingdom. As institution, teaching, ritual, the Church is indeed not only *in* this world, but also *of* this world, a "part" of it. It is the Holy Spirit whose *coming* is the inauguration, the manifestation of the ultimate, of the "last things," who transforms the Church into the "sacrament" of the Kingdom, makes her life the presence, in this world, of the world to come.

Confirmation is thus the personal Pentecost of man, his entrance into the new life in the Holy Spirit, which is the true life of the Church. It is his ordination as truly and fully man, for to be fully man is precisely to belong to the Kingdom of God. And again, it is not his "soul" alone—his "spiritual" or "religious" life—that is thus confirmed, but the totality of his human being. His whole body is anointed, sealed, sanctified, *dedicated* to the new life: "The seal of the gift of the Holy Spirit," says the Priest as he anoints the newly baptized, "on the brow, and on the eyes, and the nostrils, and the lips, and on both ears, and the breast and on the hands, and the feet." The whole man is now made the temple of God, and his whole life is from now on a *liturgy.* It is here, at this moment, that the pseudo-Christian opposition of the "spiritual" and the "material," the "sacred" and the "profane," the "religious" and the "secular" is denounced, abolished, and revealed as a monstrous lie about God and man and the world. The only true temple of God is man and through man the world. Each ounce of matter belongs to God and is to find in God its fulfillment. Each instant of time is God's time and is to fulfill itself as God's eternity. Nothing is "neutral." For the Holy Spirit, as a ray of light, as a smile of joy, has "touched" all things, all time—revealing all of them as precious stones of a precious temple.

To be truly man means to be fully *oneself.* The confirmation is the confirmation of man in his own, unique "personality." It is, to use again the same image, his ordination to be *himself,* to become what God wants him to be, what He has loved in me from all eternity. It is the gift of vocation. If the Church is truly the "newness of life"—the world and nature as restored in Christ—it is not, or rather ought not be, a purely religious institution in which to be "pious," to be a member in "good standing," means leaving one's own personality at the entrance—in the "check room"—and replacing it with a worn-out, impersonal, neutral "good Christian" type personality. Piety in fact may be a very dangerous thing, a real opposition to the Holy Spirit who is the Giver of *Life*—of joy, movement and creativity—and not of the "good conscience" which looks at everything with suspicion, fear and moral indignation.

Confirmation is the opening of man to the wholeness of divine creation, to the true *catholicity* of life. This is the "wind," the *ruah* of God entering our life, embracing it with fire and love, making us available for divine action, filling everything with joy and hope. . . .

5

We have already mentioned that in the past baptism took place on Easter—as part of the great Paschal celebration. Its natural fulfillment was thus, of course, the entrance of the newly baptized into the Eucharist of the Church, the sacrament of our participation in the *Pascha* of the Kingdom. For baptism opens the doors of the Kingdom and the Holy Spirit leads us into its joy and peace, and this means into the eucharistic fulfillment. Even today, baptism and confirmation are immediately followed by a procession —which now has the form of a circular procession around the baptismal font. Originally, however, it was the procession to the doors of the Church, the procession of the entrance. It is significant that the Introit hymn of the Paschal liturgy is the same which we sing as we lead the "neophyte" in the baptismal procession: "As many as have been baptized into Christ, have put on Christ. Allelulia!" It is baptism, it is the baptismal Pentecost that originates the Church as procession, as entrance, as ascension into the eternal *Pascha* of the Lord.

And then, for *eight* days—the image of the fullness of time—the newly baptized were in the church, and each of those days was celebrated as Easter. On the eighth day took place the rite of the washing off of the holy chrism, the cutting of hair, and the return into the world. From the fullness of time and joy into the time of the world as witnesses and bearers of that joy—such is the meaning of these rites, identical to the meaning of the eucharistic dismissal, "Let us go forth in peace." The visible signs of the sacrament are washed off—the "symbol" is to become reality, the life itself is now to be the sacramental sign, the fulfillment of the gift. And the cutting of hair—the last rite of the baptismal liturgy—is. the sign that the life which now begins is a life of offering and sacrifice, the life constantly transformed into the *liturgy*—the *work* of Christ.

6

It is only in the light of baptism that we can understand the sacramental character attached by the Orthodox Church to *penance*. In its juridical deviation, sacramental theology

explained this sacrament in terms of sheer "juridical" power
to absolve sins, a power "delegated" by Christ to the priest.
But this explanation has nothing to do with the original
meaning of penance in the Church, and with its sacramental nature. The sacrament of forgiveness is baptism, not
because it operates a juridical removal of guilt, but because
it is *baptism into Jesus Christ,* who is the Forgiveness. The
sin of all sins—the truly "original sin"—is not a transgres-
sion of rules, but, first of all, the deviation of man's love
and his alienation from God. That man prefers something—the world, himself—to God, this is the only real sin,
and in it all sins become natural, inevitable. This sin destroys
the true life of man. It deviates life's course from its only
meaning and direction. And in Christ this sin is forgiven,
not in the sense that God now has "forgotten" it and pays
no attention to it, but because in Christ man has *returned*
to God, and has returned to God because he has loved Him
and found in Him the only true object of love and life. And
God has accepted man and—in Christ—reconciled him with
Himself. Repentance is thus the return of our love, of our
life, to God, and this return is possible in Christ because
He reveals to us the true Life and makes us aware of our
exile and condemnation. To believe in Christ is to *repent*—
to change radically the very "mind" of our life, to see
it as sin and death. And to believe in Him is to *accept* the
joyful revelation that in Him forgiveness and reconciliation
have been given. In baptism both repentance and forgiveness
find their fulfillment. In baptism man *wants* to die as a
sinful man and he is given that death, and in baptism man
wants the newness of life as forgiveness, and he is given it.

And yet sin is still in us and we constantly fall away from
the new life we have received. The fight of the new Adam
against the old Adam is a long and painful one, and what a
naive oversimplification it is to think, as some do, that the
"salvation" they experience in revivals and "decisions for
Christ," and which result in moral righteousness, soberness
and warm philanthropy, is the whole of salvation, is what
God meant when He gave His Son for the life of the world.
The one true sadness is "that of not being a saint," and how

often the "moral" Christians are precisely those who never feel, never experience this sadness, because their own "experience of salvation," the feeling of "being saved" fills them with self-satisfaction; and whoever has been "satisfied" has received already his reward and cannot thirst and hunger for that total transformation and transfiguration of life which alone makes "saints."

Baptism is forgiveness of sins, not their removal. It introduces the sword of Christ into our life and makes it the real conflict, the inescapable pain and suffering of growth. It is indeed after baptism and because of it, that the reality of sin can be recognized in all its sadness, and true repentance becomes possible. Therefore, the whole of the Church is at the same time the gift of forgiveness, the joy of the "world to come," and also and inescapably a constant repentance. The *feast* is impossible without the *fast,* and the fast is precisely repentance and return, the saving experience of sadness and exile. The Church is the gift of the Kingdom—yet it is this very gift that makes obvious our absence from the Kingdom, our alienation from God. It is repentance that takes us again and again into the joy of the Paschal banquet, but it is that joy which reveals to us our sinfulness and puts us under judgment.

The *sacrament* of *penance* is not, therefore, a sacred and juridical "power" given by God to men. It is the power of baptism as it lives in the Church. From baptism it receives its sacramental character. In Christ all sins are forgiven once and for all, for He is Himself the forgiveness of sins, and there is no need for any "new" absolution. But there is indeed the need for us who constantly *leave* Christ and *excommunicate* ourselves from His life, to return to Him, to receive again and again the gift which in Him has been given once and for all. And the absolution is the sign that this return has taken place and has been fulfilled. Just as each Eucharist is not a "repetition" of Christ's supper but our ascension, our acceptance into the same and eternal banquet, so also the sacrament of penance is not a repetition of baptism, but our return to the "newness of life" which God gave to us once and for all.

5

The Mystery of Love

"This is a great mystery: but I speak concerning Christ and the Church" (Eph. 5:32)

In the Orthodox Church matrimony is a sacrament. It may be asked why, of the many "states" of human life, in the great variety of man's vocations, only this "state" has been singled out and understood as a sacrament? Indeed, if it is simply a divine *sanction* of marriage, the bestowing of spiritual help to the married couple, a blessing for the procreation of children—all this does not make it radically different from any other act for which we need help and guidance, sanction and blessing. For a "sacrament," as we have seen, implies necessarily the idea of transformation, refers to the ultimate event of Christ's death and resurrection, and is always a sacrament of the Kingdom. In a way, of course, the whole life of the Church can be termed sacramental, for it is always the manifestation in time of the "new time." Yet in a more precise way the Church calls sacraments those decisive acts of its life in which this transforming grace is *confirmed as being given,* in which the Church through a liturgical act identifies itself with and becomes the very form of that Gift. . . . But how is marriage related to the Kingdom which is to come? How is it related to the cross, the death and the resurrection of Christ? What, in other words, makes it a sacrament?

Even to raise these questions seems impossible within the whole "modern" approach to marriage, and this includes, often enough, the "Christian" approach. In the numberless "manuals of marital happiness," in the alarming trend to make the minister a specialist in clinical sexology, in all cozy definitions of a Christian family which approve a moderate use of sex (which can be an "enriching experience") and emphasize responsibility, savings and Sunday School—in all this there is, indeed, no room for sacrament. We do not even remember today that marriage is, as everything else in "this world," a fallen and distorted marriage, and that it needs not to be blessed and "solemnized"—after a rehearsal and with the help of the photographer—but *restored*. This restoration, furthermore, is *in Christ* and this means in His life, death, resurrection and ascension to heaven, in the pentecostal inauguration of the "new eon," in the Church as the sacrament of all this. Needless to say, this restoration infinitely transcends the idea of the "Christian family," and gives marriage cosmic and universal dimensions.

Here is the whole point. As long as we visualize marriage as the concern of those alone who are being married, as something that happens to them and not to the whole Church, and, therefore, to the world itself, we shall never understand the truly sacramental meaning of marriage: the great mystery to which St. Paul refers when he says, "But I speak concerning Christ and the Church." We must understand that the real theme, "content" and object of this sacrament is not "family," but love. Family as such, family in itself, can be a demonic distortion of love—and there are harsh words about it in the Gospel: "A man's foes shall be those of his own household" (Mt. 10:36). In this sense the sacrament of matrimony is wider than family. It is the sacrament of divine love, as the all-embracing mystery of being itself, and it is for this reason that it concerns the whole Church, and—through the Church—the whole world.

2

Perhaps the Orthodox vision of this sacrament will be better understood if we begin not with matrimony as such, and not with an abstract "theology of love," but with the one who has always stood at the very heart of the Church's life as the purest expression of human love and response to God—Mary, the Mother of Jesus. It is significant that whereas in the West Mary is primarily the *Virgin,* a being almost totally different from us in her absolute and celestial purity and freedom from all carnal pollution, in the East she is always referred to and glorified as *Theotokos,* the Mother of God, and virtually all icons depict her with the Child in her arms. There exist, in other words, two emphases in mariology, which, although they do not necessarily exclude one another, lead to two different visions of Mary's place in the Church. And the difference between them must be kept in mind if we want to understand the experience of the veneration of Mary which has always been that of the Orthodox Church. We hope to show that this is not so much a specific "cult of Mary," as a light, a joy, proper to the whole life of the Church. In her, says an Orthodox hymn, "all creation rejoices."

But what is this joy about? Why, in her own words, shall "all generations call me blessed"? Because in her love and obedience, in her faith and humility, she accepted to be what from all eternity all creation was meant and created to be: the temple of the Holy Spirit, the *humanity* of God. She accepted to give her body and blood—that is, her whole life—to be the body and blood of the Son of God, to be *mother* in the fullest and deepest sense of this world, giving her life to the Other and fulfilling her life in Him. She accepted the only true nature of each creature and all creation: to place the-meaning and, therefore, the fulfillment of her life in God.

In accepting this nature she fulfilled the *womanhood* of creation. This word will seem strange to many. In our time the Church, following the modern trend toward the "equality of the sexes," uses only one-half of the Christian revelation about man and woman, the one which affirms that in Christ there is neither "male nor female" (Gal. 3:28). The other half is ascribed again to an antiquated world view. In fact, however, all our attempts to find the "place of woman" in society (or in the Church) instead of exalting her, belittle woman, for they imply too often a denial of her specific vocation as woman.

Yet is it not significant that the relation between God and the world, between God and Israel, His chosen people, and finally between God and the cosmos restored in the Church, is expressed in the Bible in terms of marital union and love? This is a double analogy. On the one hand we understand God's love for the world and Christ's love for the Church because we have the experience of marital love, but on the other hand marital love has its roots, its depth and real fulfillment in the *great mystery of Christ and his Church*: "But I speak concerning Christ and the Church." The Church is the Bride of Christ (". . . for I have espoused you to one husband, that I may present you as a chaste virgin to Christ"—2 Cor. 11:2). This means that the world—which finds its restoration and fulfillment in the Church—is the bride of God and that in sin this fundamental relationship has been broken, distorted. And it is in Mary—the Woman, the Virgin, the Mother—in her response to God, that the Church has its living and personal beginning.

This response is total obedience in love; not obedience *and* love, but the wholeness of the one as the totality of the other. Obedience, taken in itself, is not a "virtue"; it is blind submission and there is no light in blindness. Only love for God, the absolute object of all love, frees obedience from blindness and makes it the joyful acceptance of that alone which is worthy of being accepted. But love without obedience to God is "the lust of the flesh, and the lust of the eyes, and the pride of life" (1 Jn. 2:16), it is the love claimed by Don Juan, which ultimately destroys him. Only obedience to God, the only Lord of Creation, gives love its true direction, makes it fully love.

True obedience is thus true love for God, the true re-

sponse of Creation to its Creator. Humanity is fully
humanity when it is this response to God, when it becomes
the movement of total self-giving and obedience to Him. But
in the "natural" world the bearer of this obedient love,
of this love as response, is the woman. The man pro-
poses, the woman accepts. This acceptance is not passivity,
blind submission, because it is love, and love is always
active. It gives life to the proposal of man, fulfills it as life,
yet it becomes fully love and fully life only when it is fully
acceptance and *response.* This is why the whole creation,
the whole Church—and not only women—find the expression
of their response and obedience to God in Mary the
Woman, and rejoice in her. She stands for all of us,
because only when we accept, respond in love and obedience—only when we accept the essential womanhood of
creation—do we become ourselves true men and women;
only then can we indeed *transcend* our limitations as
"males" and "females." For man can be truly man—that
is, the king of creation, the priest and minister of God's
creativity and initiative—only when he does not posit
himself as the "owner" of creation and submits himself—
in obedience and love—to its nature as the bride of God,
in *response* and *acceptance.* And woman ceases to be just
a "female" when, totally and unconditionally accepting
the life of the Other as *her own life,* giving herself totally
to the Other, she becomes the very expression, the very
fruit, the very joy, the very beauty, the very gift of our
response to God, the one whom, in the words of the Song,
the king will bring into his chambers, saying: "Thou art
all fair, my love, there is no spot in thee" (Ct. 4:7).

Tradition calls Mary the *new Eve.* She did what the
first Eve failed to do. Eve failed to be a woman. She took
the initiative. She "proposed," and she became "female"—
the instrument of procreation, "ruled over" by man. She
made herself, and also the man whose "eve" she was, the
slaves of her "femininity" and the whole of life a dark
war of sexes in which "possession" is in fact the violent
and desperate desire to *kill* the shameful lust that never
dies. But Mary "took no initiative." In love and obedience

she expected the initiative of the Other. And when it came, she accepted it, not blindly—for she asked "how shall this be?"—but with the whole lucidity, simplicity and joy of love. The light of an eternal spring comes to us when on the day of annunciation we hear the decisive: "Behold the handmaid of the Lord, be it unto me according to thy word" (Lk. 1:38). This is indeed the whole creation, all of humanity, and each one of us recognizing the words that express our ultimate nature and being, our acceptance to be the bride of God, our betrothal to the One who from all eternity loved us.

Mary is the *Virgin*. But this virginity is not a negation, not a mere *absence;* it is the fullness and the wholeness of love itself. It is the totality of her self-giving to God, and thus the very expression, the very quality of her love. For love is the thirst and hunger for wholeness, totality, fulfillment—for virginity, in the ultimate meaning of this word. At the end the Church will be presented to Christ as a "chaste virgin" (Cor. 11:2). For virginity is the goal of all genuine love—not as absence of "sex," but as its complete fulfillment in love; of this fulfillment in "this world" sex is the paradoxical, the tragic affirmation and denial. The Orthodox Church, by celebrating the seemingly "nonscriptural" feasts of Mary's nativity and of her presentation in the temple reveals, in fact, a real faithfulness to the Bible, for the meaning of these feasts lies precisely in their recognition of the Virgin Mary as the *goal* and the *fulfillment* of the whole history of salvation, of that history of love and obedience, of response and expectation. She is the true daughter of the Old Testament, its last and most beautiful flower. The Orthodox Church rejects the dogma of the Immaculate Conception precisely because it makes Mary a miraculous "break" in this long and patient growth of love and expectation, of this "hunger for the living God" which fills the Old Testament. She is the gift of the world to God, as is so beautifully said in a hymn of the nativity:

> Each of thy creatures brings thanksgiving unto Thee;
> The angels offer the sun,

> The heavens its star,
> The wise men their gifts,
> The shepherds their marveling . . .
> And we—the Virgin Mother.

And yet it is God alone who fulfils and crowns this obedience, acceptance, and love. "The Holy Ghost shall come upon thee and the power of the Highest shall overshadow thee.   For with God nothing shall be impossible" (Lk. 1:35—37). He alone reveals as Virgin the one who brought to him the totality of human love. . . .

Mary is the *Mother*. Motherhood is the fulfillment of womanhood because it is the fulfillment of love as obedience and response. It is by giving herself that love gives life, becomes the source of life. One does not love *in order* to have children. Love needs no justification; it is not because it gives life that love is good: it is because it is good that it gives life. The joyful mystery of Mary's motherhood is thus not opposed to the mystery of her virginity. It is the same mystery. She is not mother "in spite" of her virginity. She reveals the fullness of motherhood because her virginity is the fullness of love.

She is the *Mother of Christ*. She is the fullness of love accepting the coming of God to us—giving life to Him, who is the Life of the world. And the whole creation rejoices in her, because it recognizes through her that the end and fulfillment of all life, of all love *is to accept Christ*, to give Him life in ourselves. And there should be no fear that this joy about Mary takes anything from Christ, diminishes in any way the glory due to Him and Him alone. For what we find in her and what constitutes the joy of the Church is precisely the fullness of our adoration of Christ, of acceptance and love for Him. Really, here is no "cult of Mary," yet in Mary the "cult" of the Church becomes a movement of joy and thanksgiving, of acceptance and obedience—the wedding to the Holy Spirit, which makes it the only complete joy on earth.

3

We now can return to the sacrament of matrimony. We can now understand that its true meaning is not that it merely gives a religious "sanction" to marriage and family life, reinforces with supernatural grace the natural family virtues. Its meaning is that by taking the "natural" marriage into "the great mystery of Christ and the Church," the sacrament of matrimony gives marriage a *new meaning;* it transforms, in fact, not only marriage as such but all human love.

It is worth mentioning that the early Church apparently did not know of any separate marriage service. The "fulfillment" of marriage by two Christians was their partaking together of the Eucharist. As every aspect of life was gathered into the Eucharist, so matrimony received its seal by inclusion into this central act of the community. And this means that, since marriage has always had sociological and legal dimensions, these were simply accepted by the Church. Yet, like the whole "natural" life of man, marriage had to be *taken into the Church,* that is, judged, redeemed and transformed in the sacrament of the Kingdom. Only later did the Church receive also the "civil" authority to perform a rite of marriage. This meant, however, together with the recognition of the Church as the "celebrant" of matrimony, a first step in a progressive "desacramentalization." An obvious sign of this was the divorce of matrimony from the Eucharist.

All this explains why even today the Orthodox rite of matrimony consists of two distinct services: the betrothal and the crowning. The betrothal is performed not inside the Church, but in the vestibule. It is the Christian form of the "natural" marriage. It is the blessing of the rings by the priest and their exchange by the bridal pair. Yet from the very beginning this natural marriage is given its true perspective and direction: "O Lord our God," says the priest, *"who hast espoused the Church as a pure Virgin* from among the Gentiles, bless this Betrothal, and unite and maintain these Thy servants in peace and oneness of mind."

For the Christian, *natural* does not mean either self-sufficient—a "nice little family"—or merely insufficient, and to be, therefore, strengthened and completed by the addition of the *"supernatural."* The natural man thirsts and hungers for fulfillment and redemption. This thirst and hunger is the *vestibule* of the Kingdom: both beginning and exile.

Then, having blessed the natural marriage, the priest takes the bridal pair in a solemn procession *into the church.* This is the true form of the sacrament, for it does not merely symbolize, but indeed *is* the entrance of marriage into the Church, which is the entrance of the world into the "world to come," the procession of the people of God —in Christ—into the Kingdom. The rite of crowning is but a later—although a beautiful and beautifully meaningful—expression of the reality of this entrance.

"O Lord and God, crown them with glory and honor!" says the priest after he has put crowns on the heads of the bridal pair. This is, first, the glory and honor of man as king of creation: "Be fruitful and multiply and replenish the earth, and subdue and have dominion . . ." (Gn. 1:25). Each family is indeed a kingdom, a little church, and therefore a sacrament of and a way to the Kingdom. Somewhere, even if it is only in a single room, every man at some point in his life has his own small kingdom. It may be hell, and a place of betrayal, or it may not. Behind each window there is a little world going on. How evident this becomes when one is riding on a train at night and passing innumerable lighted windows: behind each one of them the fullness of life is a "given possibility," a promise, a vision. This is what the marriage crowns express: that here is the beginning of a small kingdom which *can* be something like the true Kingdom. The chance will be lost, perhaps even in one night; but at this moment it is still an open possibility. Yet even when it has been lost, and lost again a thousand times, still if two people stay together, they are in a real sense king and queen to each other. And after forty odd years, Adam can still turn and see Eve standing beside him, in a unity with himself which in some small way at least proclaims the love of God's Kingdom. In movies and magazines the "icon" of marriage is always a youthful couple. But once, in the light and warmth of an autumn afternoon, this writer saw on the bench of a public square, in a poor Parisian suburb, an old and poor couple. They were sitting hand in hand, in silence, enjoying the pale light, the last warmth of the season. In silence: all words had been said, all passion exhausted, all storms at peace. The whole life was behind—yet all of it was now *present,* in this silence, in this light, in this warmth, in this silent unity of hands. Present—and ready for eternity, ripe for joy. This to me remains the vision of marriage, of its heavenly beauty.

Then secondly, the glory and the honor is that of the martyr's crown. For the way to the Kingdom is the *martyria* —bearing witness to Christ. And this means crucifixion and suffering. A marriage which does not constantly crucify its own selfishness and self-sufficiency, which does not "die to itself" that it may point beyond itself, is not a Christian marriage. The real sin of marriage today is not adultery or lack of "adjustment" or "mental cruelty." It is the idolization of the family itself, the refusal to understand marriage as directed toward the Kingdom of God. This is expressed in the sentiment that one would "do anything" for his family, even steal. The family has here ceased to be for the glory of God; it has ceased to be a sacramental entrance into His presence. It is not the lack of respect for the family, it is the idolization of the family that breaks the modern family so easily, making divorce its almost natural shadow. It is the identification of marriage with happiness and the refusal to accept the cross in it. In a Christian marriage, in fact, three are married; and the united loyalty of the two toward the third, who is God, keeps the two in an active unity with each other as well as with God. Yet it is the presence of God which is the death of the marriage as something only "natural." It is the cross of Christ that brings the self-sufficiency of nature to

its end. But "by the cross joy [and not 'happiness!']
entered the whole world." Its presence is thus the real
joy of marriage. It is the joyful certitude that the marriage
vow, in the perspective of the eternal Kingdom, is not
taken "until death parts," but until death unites us completely.

Hence the third and final meaning of the crowns: they
are the crowns of the Kingdom, of that ultimate Reality
of which everything in "this world"—whose fashion passeth away—everything has now become a sacramental sign
and anticipation. "Receive their crowns in Thy Kingdom,"
says the priest, as he removes them from the heads of the
newlyweds, and this means: make this marriage a growth
in that perfected love of which God alone is the end and
fullness.

The common cup given to the couple after the crowning
is explained today as a symbol of "common life," and
nothing shows better the "desacramentalization" of marriage, its reduction to a "natural happiness." In the past
this was communion, the partaking of the Eucharist, the
ultimate *seal* of the fulfillment of marriage in Christ. Christ
is to be the very essence of life together. He is the wine of
the new life of the children of God, and communion in it
will proclaim how, by getting older and older in this
world, we are growing younger and younger in the life
which has no evening.

As the wedding service is completed, the bride and
bridegroom join hands and follow the priest in a procession
around the table. As in baptism, this procession in a circle
signifies the eternal journey which has begun; marriage
will be a procession hand in hand, a continuation of that
which has started here, not always joyful, but always
capable of being referred to and filled with joy.

4

Nowhere is the truly universal, truly cosmic significance
of the sacrament of matrimony as the sacrament of love,

expressed better than in its liturgical similitude with the liturgy of ordination, the sacrament of priesthood. Through it is revealed the identity of the Reality to which both sacraments refer, of which both are the manifestation.

Centuries of "clericalism" (and one should not think of clericalism as a monopoly of the "hierarchical" and "liturgical" churches) have made the priest or minister *beings apart*, with a unique and specifically "sacred" vocation in the Church. This vocation is not only different from, it is indeed opposed to all of those that are "profane." Such was, such still is the secret spring of sacerdotal psychology and training. It is not accidental, therefore, that the words "laity," "layman" became little by little synonymous with a lack of something in a man, or his *nonbelonging*. Yet originally the words "laity," "layman" referred to the *laos*—the people of God—and were not only positive in meaning, but included the "clergy." But today one who says he is a layman in physics acknowledges his ignorance of this science, his nonbelonging to the closed circle of specialists.

For centuries the clerical state was exalted as virtually a "supernatural" one, and there is a slight connotation of mystical awe when a man says: "People should respect the clergy." And if someday a science which has been long overdue—pastoral pathology—is taught in the seminaries, its first discovery might be that some "clerical vocations" are in fact rooted in a morbid desire for that "supernatural respect," especially when the chances of a "natural" one are slim. Our secular world "respects" clergy as it "respects" cemeteries: both are needed, both are sacred, both are out of life.

But what both clericalism and secularism—the former being, in fact, the natural father of the latter—have made us forget is that to be *priest* is from a profound point of view the most natural thing in the world. Man was created priest of the world, the one who offers the world to God in a sacrifice of love and praise and who, through this eternal eucharist, bestows the divine love upon the world. Priesthood, in this sense, is the very essence of manhood, man's creative relation to the "womanhood" of the created world. And Christ is the one true Priest because He is the one true and perfect man. He is the new Adam, the restoration of that which Adam failed to be. Adam failed to be the priest of the world, and because of this failure the world ceased to be the sacrament of the divine love and presence, and became "nature." And in this "natural" world religion became an organized transaction with the supernatural, and the priest was set apart as the "transactor," as the mediator between the natural and the supernatural. And after all, it does not matter too much whether this mediation was understood in terms of magic—as supernatural powers—or in terms of law—as supernatural rights.

But Christ revealed the essence of priesthood to be love and therefore priesthood to be the essence of life. He died the last victim of the priestly religion, and in His death the priestly *religion* died and the priestly *life* was inaugurated. He was killed by the priests, by the "clergy," but His sacrifice abolished them as it abolished "religion." And it abolished religion because *it* destroyed that wall of separation between the "natural" and the "supernatural," the "profane" and the "sacred," the "this-worldly" and the "other-worldly"—which was the only justification and *raison d'etre* of religion. He revealed that all things, all nature have their end, their fulfillment in the Kingdom; that all things are to be made new by love.

If there are priests in the Church, if there is the priestly vocation in it, it is precisely in order to reveal to. each vocation its priestly essence, to make the whole life of all men the liturgy of the Kingdom, to reveal the Church as the royal priesthood of the redeemed world. It is, in other terms, not a vocation "apart," but the expression of love for man's vocation as son of God and for the world as the sacrament of the Kingdom. And there must be priests because we live in *this world,* and nothing in it is the Kingdom and, as "this world," will never become the Kingdom. The Church is in the world but not of the world, because only by *not* being of the world can it reveal and manifest the "world to come," the beyond, which alone reveals all things as *old*—yet new and eternal in the love of God.

Therefore, no vocation in *this world* can fulfill itself as priesthood. And thus there must be the one whose specific vocation is *to have no vocation, to be all things to all men,* and to reveal that the end and the meaning of all things are in Christ.

No one can take it upon himself to become a priest, to decide on the basis of his own qualifications, preparation and predispositions. The vocation always comes from above —from God's ordination and order. The priesthood reveals the humility, not the pride of the Church, for it reveals the complete dependence of the Church on Christ's love— that is, on His unique and perfect priesthood. It is not "priesthood" that the priest receives in his ordination, but the gift of Christ's love, that love which made Christ the only Priest and which fills with this unique priesthood the ministry of those whom He sends to His people.

This is why the sacrament of ordination is, in a sense, identical with the sacrament of matrimony. Both are manifestations of love. The priest is indeed married to the Church. But just as the human marriage is taken into the mystery of Christ and the Church and becomes the sacrament of the Kingdom, it is this marriage of the priest with the Church that makes him really *priest,* the true minister of that Love which alone transforms the world and reveals the Church as the immaculate bride of Christ.

The final point is this: some of us are married and some are not. Some of us are called to be priests and ministers and some are not. But the sacraments of matrimony and priesthood *concern* all of us, because they concern our life as *vocation.* The meaning, the essence and the end of all vocation is *the mystery of Christ and the Church.* It is through the Church that each one of us finds that the vocation of all vocations is to follow Christ in the fullness of His priesthood: in His love for man and the world, His love for their ultimate fulfillment in the abundant life of the Kingdom.

6

Trampling Down Death by Death

We live today in a death-denying culture. This is clearly seen in the unobtrusive appearance of the ordinary funeral home, in its attempt to look like all other houses. Inside, the "funeral director" tries to take care of things in such a way that one will not notice that one is sad; and a parlor ritual is designed to transform a funeral into a semi-pleasant experience. There is a strange conspiracy of silence concerning the blunt fact of death, and the corpse itself is "beautified" so as to disguise its deadness. But there existed in the past and there still exist—even within our life-affirming modern world—"death-centered" cultures, in which death is the one great all-embracing preoccupation, and life itself is conceived as being mainly preparation for death. If to some the funeral home itself seems to divert thoughts from death, to some others even the "utilities" such as a bed or a table become symbols, reminders of death. A bed is seen as the image of the grave, the casket is put on the table.

Where is Christianity in all this? There can be no doubt, on the one hand, that the "problem of death" is central and essential in its message, which announces Christ's victory over death, and that Christianity has its source in that victory. Yet, on the other hand, one has the strange feeling that although this message has certainly been heard, it has

95

had no real impact on the basic human attitudes toward death. It is rather Christianity that has "adjusted" itself to these attitudes, accepted them as its own. It is not difficult to dedicate to God—in a nice Christian sermon—new skyscrapers and world's fairs, to join—if not to lead—the great progressive and life-affirming forces of our "atomic age," to make Christianity appear as the very source of all this hectic and life-centered activity. And it is equally easy, when preaching at a funeral or a retreat, to present life as a valley of suffering and vanity, and to present death as a liberation.

A Christian minister, representative in this of the whole Church, must today use *both languages,* espouse both attitudes. But if he is sincere he must inescapably feel that "something is missing" in both, and that this is in fact *the Christian element itself.* For it falsifies the Christian message to present and to preach Christianity as essentially life-affirming—without referring this affirmation to the death of Christ and therefore to the very fact of death; to pass over in silence the fact that for Christianity death is not only the end, but indeed the very reality of *this world.* But to "comfort" people and reconcile them with death by making this world a meaningless scene of an individual preparation for death is also to falsify it. For Christianity proclaims that Christ died for the life of the world, and not for an "eternal rest" from it. This "falsification" makes the very success of Christianity (according to official data church building and per capita contributions to churches have reached an all time high!) into a profound tragedy. The worldly man wants the minister to be an optimistic fellow, sanctioning faith in an optimistic and progressive world. And the religious man sees him as an utterly serious, sadly solemn and dignified denouncer of the world's vanity and futility. The world does not want religion and religion does not want Christianity. The one rejects death, the other, life. Hence the immense frustration either with the secularistic tendencies of the life-affirming world or with the morbid religiosity of those who oppose it.

This frustration will last as long as Christians continue

to understand Christianity as a religion whose purpose is to *help*, as long as they continue to keep the "utilitarian" self-consciousness typical of the "old religion." For this was, indeed, one of the main functions of religions: to help, and especially to help people to die. For this reason religion has always been an attempt to *explain* death, and by explaining it, to reconcile man with it. What pains Plato took in his *Phaedo* to make death desirable and even good, and how often he has since been echoed in the history of human belief when confronted with the prospect of release from this world of change and suffering! Men have consoled themselves with the rationalization that God made death and that it is therefore right, or with the fact that death belongs to the pattern of life; they have found various meanings in death, or assured themselves that death is preferable to decrepit old age; they have formulated doctrines of the immortality of the soul—that if a man dies, at least a part of him survives. All this has been one long attempt to take the awful uniqueness out of the experience of death.

Christianity, because it is a *religion*, had to accept this fundamental function of religion: to "justify" death and thus to *help*. In doing so, moreover, it more or less assimilated the old and classical explanations of death, common to virtually all religions. For neither the doctrine of the immortality of the soul, based on the opposition between the spiritual and the material, nor that of death as liberation, nor of death as punishment, are, in fact, Christian doctrines. And their integration into the Christian world view vitiated rather than clarified Christian theology and piety. They "worked" as long as Christianity lived in a "religious" (i.e., death-centered) world. But they ceased to work as soon as the world outgrew this old death-centered religion and became "secular." Yet the world has become secular not because it has become "irreligious," "materialistic," "superficial," not because it has "lost religion"— as so many Christians still think—but because old explanations do not really explain. Christians often do not realize that they themselves, or rather Christianity, has been a major factor in this liberation from the old religion. Christianity, with its message offering fullness of life, has contributed more than anything else to the liberation of man from the fears and the pessimism of religion. Secularism, in this sense, is a phenomenon within the Christian world, a phenomenon impossible without Christianity. Secularism rejects Christianity insofar as Christianity has identified itself with the "old religion" and is forcing upon the world those "explanations" and "doctrines" of death and life which Christianity has itself destroyed.

It would be a great mistake, however, to think of secularism as simply an "absence of religion." It is, in fact, itself a religion, and as such, an explanation of death and a reconciliation with it. It is the religion of those who are tired of having the world explained in terms of an "other world" of which no one knows anything, and life explained in terms of a "survival" about which no one has the slightest idea; tired of having, in other words, life given "value" in terms of death. Secularism is an "explanation" of death in terms of life. The only world we know is this world, the only life given to us is this life—so thinks a secularist—and it is up to us men to make it as meaningful, as rich, as happy as possible. Life ends with death. This is unpleasant, but since it is natural, since death is a universal phenomenon, the best thing man can do about it is simply to accept it as something natural. As long as he lives, however, he need not think about it, but should live as though death did not exist. The best way to forget about death is to be busy, to be useful, to be dedicated to great and noble things, to build an always better world. If God exists (and a great many secularists firmly believe in God and the usefulness of religion for their corporate and individual enterprises) and if He, in His love and mercy (for we all have our shortcomings) wants to reward us for our busy, useful and righteous life with eternal vacations, traditionally called "immortality," it is strictly His gracious business. But immortality is an appendix (however eternal) to this life, in which all real interests, all true values are to be found. The American "funeral home" is indeed the very symbol

of secularist religion, for it expresses both the quiet acceptance of death as something natural (a house among
other houses with nothing typical about it) and the denial
of death's *presence* in life.

Secularism is a religion because it has a faith, it has its
own eschatology and its own ethics. And it "works" and it
"helps." Quite frankly, if "help" were the criterion, one
would have to admit that life-centered secularism *helps*
actually more than religion. To compete with it, religion
has to present itself as "adjustment to life," "counselling,"
"enrichment," it has to be publicized in subways and buses
as a valuable addition to "your friendly bank" and all other
"friendly dealers": try it, it *helps!* And the religious success
of secularism is so great that it leads some Christian theologians to "give up" the very category of "transcendence,"
or in much simpler words, the very idea of "God." This is
the price we must pay if we want to be "understood" and
"accepted" by modern man, proclaim the Gnostics of the
twentieth century.

But it is here that we reach the heart of the matter. For
Christianity *help* is not the criterion. Truth is the criterion.
The purpose of Christianity is not to help people by recon-
ciling them with death, but to reveal the Truth about life
and death in order that people may be saved by this Truth.
Salvation, however, is not only not identical with help, but
is, in fact, opposed to it. Christianity quarrels with religion
and secularism not because they offer "insufficient help,"
but precisely because they "suffice," because they "satisfy"
the needs of men. If the purpose of Christianity were to
take away from man the fear of death, to reconcile him
with death, there would be no need for Christianity, for
other religions have done this, indeed, better than Christianity. And secularism is about to produce men who will
gladly and corporately die—and not just live—for the
triumph of the Cause, whatever it may be.

Christianity is not reconciliation with death. It is the
revelation of death, and it reveals death because it is the
revelation of Life. Christ is this Life. And only if Christ is
Life is death what Christianity proclaims it to be, namely

the enemy to be destroyed, and not a "mystery" to be explained. Religion and secularism, by explaining death, give
it a "status," a rationale, make it "normal." Only Christianity proclaims it to be *abnormal* and, therefore, truly hor-
rible. At the grave of Lazarus Christ wept, and when His
own hour to die approached, "he began to be sore amazed
and very heavy." In the light of Christ, *this* world, this *life*
are lost and are beyond mere "help," not because there is
fear of death in them, but because they have accepted and
normalized death. To accept God's world as a cosmic cemetery which is to be abolished and replaced by an "other
world" which looks like a cemetery ("eternal rest") and to
call this religion, to live in a cosmic cemetery and to "dispose" every day of thousands of corpses and to get excited
about a "just society" and to be happy!—this is the fall of
man. It is not the immorality or the crimes of man that
reveal him as a fallen being; it is his "positive ideal"—
religious or secular—and his satisfaction with this ideal.
This fall, however, can be truly revealed only by Christ,
because only in Christ is the *fullness of life* revealed to us,
and death, therefore, becomes "awful," the very fall from
life, the enemy. It is *this world* (and not any "other world"),
it is *this life* (and not some "other life") that were given
to man to be a sacrament of the divine presence, given as
communion with God, and it is only through this world,
this life, by "transforming" them into communion with
God that man *was to be*. The horror of death is, therefore, not
in its being the "end" and not in physical destruction.
By being separation from the world and life, it is *separation from God*. The dead cannot glorify God. It is, in other
words, when Christ reveals Life to us that we can hear the
Christian message about death as the enemy of God. It is
when Life weeps at the grave of the friend, when it contem-
plates the horror of death, that the victory over death begins.

2

Before death, however, there is *dying*: the growth of death in us by physical decay and illness. Here again the Christian approach cannot be simply identified either with that of the modern world, or with the one that characterizes "religion." For the modern secular world, health is the only *normal* state of man; disease therefore is to be fought, and the modern world fights it very well indeed. Hospitals and medicine are among its best achievements. Yet health has a limit, and it is death. There comes a time when the "resources of science" are exhausted—and this the modern world accepts as simply, as lucidly as it accepts death itself. There comes a moment when the patient is to be surrendered to death, to be removed from the ward, and this is done quietly, properly, hygienically—as part of the general routine. As long as a man is alive everything is to be done to keep him alive, and even if his case is hopeless, it must not be revealed to him. Death must never be part of life. And although everyone knows that people die in hospitals, their general tone and ethos are those of cheerful optimism. The object of modern medicine's efficient care is life, and not mortal life.

The religious outlook considers disease rather than health to be the "normal" state of man. In this world of mortal and changing matter suffering, sickness and sorrow are the normal conditions of life. Hospitals and medical care must be supplied, but as a religious duty and not because of any real interest in health as such. Health and healing are always thought of as the mercy of God, from the religious point of view, and real healing is "miraculous." And this miracle is performed by God, again not because health is good, but because it "proves" the power of God and brings men back to God.

In their ultimate implications these two approaches are incompatible, and nothing reveals better the confusion of Christians on this issue than the fact that today Christians accept both of them as equally valid and true. The problem of a secular hospital is solved by establishing a Christian chaplaincy in it, and the problem of a Christian hospital by making it as modern and scientific—that is, as "secular"— as possible. In fact, however, there is a progressive surrender

of the religious approach to the secular, for reasons which we
have already analyzed above. The modern minister tends to
become not only an "assistant" to the medical doctor, but
a "therapist" in his own right. All kinds of techniques of
pastoral therapy, hospital visiting, care of the sick—which
fill the catalogues of theological seminaries—are a good indication of this. But is this *the Christian* approach—and if
it is not, are we simply to return to the old—the "religious"
one?

The answer is no, it is not; but we are not simply to
"return." We must discover the unchanging, yet always
contemporary, *sacramental* vision of man's life, and therefore of his suffering and disease—the vision that has been
the Church's, even if we Christians have forgotten or misunderstood it.

The Church considers *healing* as a sacrament. But such
was its misunderstanding during the long centuries of the
total identification of the Church with "religion" (a misunderstanding from which all sacraments suffered, and the
whole doctrine of sacraments) that the *sacrament of oil*
became in fact the sacrament of death, one of the "last
rites" opening to man a more or less safe passage into
eternity. There is a danger that today, with the growing
interest in healing among Christians, it will be understood
as a sacrament of health, a useful "complement" to secular
medicine. And both views are wrong, because both miss
precisely the sacramental nature of this act.

A sacrament—as we already know—is always a *passage,*
a *transformation.* Yet it is not a "passage" into "supernature," but into the Kingdom of God, the world to come,
into the very reality of this world and its life as redeemed
and restored by Christ. It is the transformation not of
"nature" into "supernature," but of the *old* into the *new.*
A sacrament therefore is not a "miracle" by which God
breaks, so to speak, the "laws of nature," but the manifestation of the ultimate Truth about the world and life, man
and nature, the Truth which is Christ.

And healing is a sacrament because its purpose or end is
not *health* as such, the restoration of physical health, but

the *entrance* of man into the life of the Kingdom, into the "joy and peace" of the Holy Spirit. In Christ everything in this world, and this means health and disease, joy and suffering, has become an ascension to, and entrance into this new life, its expectation and anticipation.

In this world suffering and disease are indeed "normal," but their very "normalcy" is abnormal. They reveal the ultimate and permanent defeat of man and of life, a defeat which no partial victories of medicine, however wonderful and truly miraculous, can ultimately overcome. But in Christ suffering is not "removed"; it is transformed into victory. The defeat *itself* becomes victory, a way, an entrance into the Kingdom, and this is the only true *healing*.

Here is a man suffering on his bed of pain and the Church comes to him to perform the sacrament of healing. For this man, as for every man in the whole world, suffering can be defeat, the way of complete surrender to darkness, despair and solitude. It can be *dying* in the very real sense of the word. And yet it can be also the ultimate victory of Man and of Life in him. The Church does not come to restore *health* in this man, simply to replace medicine when medicine has exhausted its own possibilities. The Church comes to take this man into the Love, the Light and the Life of Christ. It comes not merely to "comfort" him in his sufferings, not to "help" him, but to make him a *martyr, a witness* to Christ in his very sufferings. A martyr is one who beholds "the heavens opened, and the Son of Man standing on the right hand of God" (Acts 7:56). A martyr is one for whom God is not another—and the last—chance to stop the awful pain; God is his very life, and thus everything in his life comes to God, and ascends to the fullness of Love.

In *this world* there shall be tribulation. Whether reduced to a minimum by man himself, or given some relief by the religious promise of a reward in the "other world," suffering remains here, it remains awfully "normal." And yet Christ says, "be of good cheer, I have overcome the world" (Jn. 16:33). Through His own suffering, not only has all suffering acquired a meaning but it has been given the power to become itself the sign, the sacrament, the proclamation, the "coming" of that victory; the defeat of man, his very *dying* has become a way of Life.

3

The beginning of this victory is Christ's death. Such is the eternal gospel, and it remains "foolishness" not only for *this world,* but also for *religion* as long as it is the religion of this world ("lest the cross of Christ should be made of no effect"—1 Cor. 1:17). The liturgy of Christian death does not begin when a man has come to the inescapable end and his corpse lies in church for the last rites while we stand around, the sad yet resigned witnesses of the dignified removal of a man from the world of the living. It begins every Sunday as the Church, ascending into heaven, "puts aside all earthly care"; it begins every feast day; it begins especially in the joy of Easter. The whole life of the Church is in a way the sacrament of our death, because all of it is the proclamation of the Lord's death, the confession of His resurrection. And yet Christianity is not a death-centered religion; it is not a "mystery cult" in which an "objective" doctrine of salvation from death is offered to me in beautiful ceremonies and requires that I believe in it and thus profit from its "benefits."

To be Christian, to believe in Christ, means and has always meant this: to know in a transrational and yet absolutely certain way called faith, that Christ is the Life of all life, that He is Life itself and, therefore, *my* life. "In him was life; and the life was the light of men." All Christian doctrines—those of the incarnation, redemption, atonement— are explanations, consequences, but not the "cause" of that faith. Only when we believe in Christ do all these affirmations become "valid" and "consistent." But faith itself is the acceptance not of this or that "proposition" about Christ, but of Christ Himself as the Life and the light of life. "For the life was manifested and we have seen it, and bear witness, and show unto you that eternal life, which was

with the Father, and was manifested unto us" (1 Jn. 1:2).
In this sense Christian faith is radically different from
"religious belief." Its starting point is not "belief" but love.
In itself and by itself all belief is partial, fragmentary,
fragile. "For we know in part, and we prophesy in part . . .
whether there be prophecies, they shall fail; whether there
be tongues, they shall cease; whether there be knowledge,
it shall vanish away." Only *love never faileth* (1 Cor. 13).
And if to love someone means that I have my life in him,
or rather that he has become the "content" of my life, to love
Christ is to know and to possess Him as the Life of my life.

Only this possession of Christ as Life, the "joy and
peace" of communion with Him, the certitude of His presence, makes meaningful the proclamation of Christ's death
and the confession of His resurrection. In *this world* Christ's
resurrection can never be made an "objective fact." The
risen Lord appeared to Mary and "she saw him standing
and knew not it was Jesus." He stood on the shore of the
Sea of Tiberias "but the disciples knew not it was Jesus."
And on the way to Emmaus the eyes of the disciples "were
holden that they should not know him." The preaching of
the resurrection remains foolishness to this world, and no
wonder even Christians themselves somehow "explain it
away" by virtually reducing it to the old pre-Christian
doctrines of immortality and survival. And indeed, if the doctrine of resurrection is just a "doctrine," if it is to be believed in as an event of the "future," as a mystery of the
"other world," it is not substantially different from the
other doctrines concerning the "other world" and can be
easily confused with them. Whether it is the immortality
of the soul or the resurrection of the body—I know nothing
of them and all discussion here is mere "speculation."
Death remains the same mysterious passage into a mysterious future. The *great joy* that the disciples felt when they
saw the risen Lord, that "burning of heart" that they experienced on the way to Emmaus were not because the mysteries
of an "other world" were revealed to them, but because
they saw the Lord. And He sent them to preach and to proclaim not the resurrection of the dead—not a doctrine of

death—but repentance and remission of sins, the new life, the Kingdom. They announced what they knew, that in Christ the *new life* has already begun, that He is Life Eternal, the Fulfillment, the Resurrection and the Joy of the world.

The Church is the entrance into the risen life of Christ; it is communion in life eternal, "joy and peace in the Holy Spirit." And it is the expectation of the "day without evening" of the Kingdom; not of any "other world," but of the fulfillment of all things and all life in Christ. In Him death itself has become an act of life, for He has filled it with Himself, with His love and light. In Him "all things are yours; whether . . . the world, or life, or death, or things present, or things to come; all are yours; and ye are Christ's; and Christ is God's" (1 Cor. 3:21—23). And if I make this *new life* mine, mine this hunger and thirst for the Kingdom, mine this expectation of Christ, mine the certitude that Christ is Life, then my very death will be an act of communion with Life. For neither life nor death can separate us from the love of Christ. I do not know when and how the fulfillment will come. I do not know when all things will be consummated in Christ. I know nothing about the "whens" and "hows." But I know that in Christ this great Passage, the *Pascha* of the world has begun, that the light of the "world to come" comes to us in the joy and peace of the Holy Spirit, for *Christ is risen and Life reigneth.*

Finally I know that it is this faith and this certitude that fill with a joyful meaning the words of St. Paul which we read each time we celebrate the "passage" of a brother, his falling asleep in Christ:

> For the Lord himself will descend from heaven with a cry of command with the archangel's call, and with the sound of the trumpet of God. And the dead in Christ will rise first; then we who are alive, who are left, shall be caught up together with them in the clouds to meet the Lord in the air; and so we shall always be with the Lord (I Thess. 4: 16-17).

7

And Ye Are Witnesses of These Things

There is no need to repeat here what has been said so often and so well in these last years: that the Church is mission and that to be mission is its very essence, its very life. There is need, however, to remind ourselves of certain "dimensions" of Christian mission that have often been forgotten since the Church accepted its *establishment* in the world, the respectable position of a "world religion."

But first, a few words about our present missionary situation. Whatever the achievements of the Christian mission in the past, today we must honestly face a double failure: the failure to achieve any substantial "victory" over the other great world religions, and the failure to overcome in any significant way the prevailing and the growing secularism of our culture. In regard to other religions Christianity stands simply as one of them, and the time is certainly gone when Christians could consider them as "primitive" and bound to disappear when exposed to the self-evident "superiority" of Christianity. Not only have they not disappeared, but they show today a remarkable vitality and they "proselytize" even within our so-called "Christian" society. As for secularism, nothing shows better our inability to cope with it than the confusion and division it provokes among Christians themselves: the total and violent rejection of secularism in all varieties of Christian "fundamentalism"

clashes with its almost enthusiastic acceptance by the numerous Christian interpreters of the "modern world" and
"modern man." Hence the unending reassessments by
Christians of their missionary task and methods, of their
place and function in the world.

Here two main streams or tendencies may be discerned.
There is, first, the *religious* approach of which we have already spoken in the first chapter. The object of mission is
thought of as the propagation of *religion,* considered to be
an essential need of man. What is significant here is that
even the most traditional, confessional and "exclusive"
churches accept the idea of a *modus vivendi* with other
religions, of all kinds of "dialogues" and "rapprochements."
There exist—such is the assumption—a basic religion, some
basic "religious" and "spiritual values," and they must be
defended against atheism, materialism and other forms of
irreligion. Not only "liberal" and "nondenominational,"
but also the most conservative Christians are ready to give
up the old idea of mission as the preaching of the one, true
universal religion, opposed as such to all other religions, and
replace it by a common front of all religions against *the
enemy*: secularism. Since all religions are threatened by its
victorious growth, since religion and the "spiritual values"
are on the decline, religious men of all faiths must forget
their quarrels and unite in defending these values.

But what are these "basic religious values"? If one ana-
lyzes them honestly, one does not find a single one that
would be "basically" different from what secularism at its
best also proclaims and offers to men. Ethics? Concern for
truth? Human brotherhood and solidarity? Justice? Abne-
gation? In all honesty, there is more passionate concern
for all these "values" among "secularists" than within the
organized religious bodies which so easily accommodate
themselves to ethical minimalism, intellectual indifference,
superstitions, dead traditionalism. What remains is the
famous "anxiety" and the numberless "personal problems"
in which religion claims to be supremely competent. But
even here is it not highly significant—and we have spoken
of this already—that when dealing with these "problems"

religion has to borrow the whole arsenal and terminology of various secular "therapeutics"? Are not, for instance, the "values" stressed in the manuals of marital happiness, both religious and secular, in fact identical, as are also the language, the images and the proposed techniques?

It sounds like a paradox, but the basic religion that is being preached and accepted as the only means of overcoming secularism is in reality a surrender to secularism. This surrender can take place—and actually does—in all Christian confessions, although it is differently "colored" in a nondenominational suburban "community church" and in a traditional, hierarchical, confessional and liturgical parish. For the surrender consists not in giving up creeds, traditions, symbols and customs (of all this the secular man, tired of his functional office, is sometimes extremely fond), but in accepting the very function of religion in terms of promoting the secular value of *help,* be it help in character building, peace of mind, or assurance of eternal salvation. It is in this "key" that religion is preached to, and accepted by, millions and millions of average believers today. And it is really amazing how little difference exists in the religious self-consciousness of members of confessions whose dogmas seem to stand in radical opposition to one another. For even if a man changes religion, it is usually because he finds the one he accepts as offering him "more help"—not more truth. While religious leaders are discussing ecumenicity at the top, there exists already at the grass roots a real ecumenicity in this "basic religion." It is here, in this "key" that we find the source of the apparent success of religions in some parts of the world, such as America, where the religious "boom" is due primarily to the secularization of religion. It is also the source of the decline of religion in those parts of the world where man has not time enough yet for constant analysis of his anxieties and where "secularism" still holds out the great promise of bread and freedom.

But if this is religion, its decline will continue, whether it takes the form of a direct abandonment of religion or that of the understanding of religion as an appendix to a world which has long ago ceased to refer itself and all its activity to God. And in this general religious decline, the non-Christian "great religions" have an even greater chance of survival. For it may be asked whether certain non-Christian "spiritual traditions" are not really of "greater help" from the standpoint of what men today expect from religion. Islam and Buddhism offer excellent religious "satisfaction" and "help" not only to primitive men, but to the most sophisticated intellectual as well. Have not Oriental *wisdom* and Oriental *mysticism* always exercised an almost irresistible attraction for religious people everywhere? It is to be feared that certain "mystical" aspects of Orthodoxy owe their growing popularity in the West precisely to their easy—although wrong—identification with Oriental mysticism. The ascetical writings collected in the *Philocalia* have a tremendous success in some esoteric groups that are supremely indifferent to the life, death, and resurrection of Jesus Christ. And the spiritual preoccupations of those esoteric groups are, in the last analysis, not very different from those of the most emphatically Christ-centered preachers of personal salvation and "assurance of life eternal." In both instances what is offered is a "spiritual dimension" of life which leaves intact and unaltered the "material dimension"—that is, the world itself—and leaves it intact without any bad conscience. It is a very serious question, indeed, whether under its seemingly traditional cover certain forms of contemporary Christian mission do not in reality pave the way for a "world religion" that will have very little in common with the faith that once overcame the world.

2

The second tendency consists in the acceptance of secularism. According to the ideologists of a "nonreligious" Christianity, secularism is not the enemy, not the fruit of man's tragic loss of religion, not a sin and a tragedy, but the world's "coming of age" which Christianity must acknowledge and accept as perfectly normal: "Honesty demands that we recognize that we must live in the world as if there were no God." This point of view has recently been developed in several remarkable books and there is no need to expound it here. The important thing for us is that mission is understood here primarily in terms of human solidarity. A Christian is a "man-for-the other." He shares completely and unconditionally in human life within a perspective conveyed to him by the story of Jesus of Nazareth. Christian mission is not to preach Christ, but to be Christians in life.

There are, no doubt, very valuable "emphases" in this trend. And first of all, secularism must indeed be acknowledged as a "Christian" phenomenon, as a result of the Christian revolution. It can be explained only within the context of the history whose starting point is the encounter between Athens and Jerusalem. It is indeed one of the grave errors of religious anti-secularism that it does not see that secularism is made up of *verites chretiennes devenues folles,* of Christian truths that "went mad," and that in simply rejecting secularism, it in fact rejects with it certain fundamentally Christian aspirations and hopes. It is true that through "secularization," and not in direct religious encounter with Christianity, men of other "great religions" can understand certain dimensions of thought and experience without which Christianity cannot be "heard." It is true also that in its historical development, Christianity has returned to the pre-Christian and fundamentally non-Christian dichotomies of the "sacred" and "profane," spiritual and material, etc., and has thus narrowed and vitiated its own message.

And yet when all this is acknowledged there remains the ultimate truth, to which the Christian partisans of secularization seem to be blind. This truth is that secularism—precisely because of its Christian "origin," because of the indelible Christian seal on it—is a *tragedy* and a *sin.* It is tragedy because having tasted a good wine, man preferred and still prefers to return to plain water; having seen the true light, he has chosen the light of his own logic. It is indeed characteristic that the prophets and the preachers of "secularized Christianity" constantly refer to "modern man" as the one who "uses electricity" and who is shaped by "industrialism" and the "scientific world view." Poetry and art, music and dancing are not included. The "modern man" has "come of age" as a deadly serious adult, conscious of his sufferings and alienations but not of joy, of sex but not of love, of science but not of "mystery." Since he knows there is no "heaven," he cannot *understand* the prayer to our Father who is in heaven, and the affirmation that heaven and earth are full of His glory. But the tragedy is also a sin, because secularism is a *lie* about the world. "To live in the world as if there were no God!"—but *honesty* to the Gospel, to the whole Christian tradition, to the experience of every saint and every word of Christian liturgy *demands* exactly the opposite: to live in the world seeing *everything* in it as a revelation of God, a sign of His presence, the joy of His coming, the call to communion with Him, the hope for fulfillment in Him. Since the day of Pentecost there is a seal, a ray, a sign of the Holy Spirit on everything for those who believe in Christ and know that He is the life of the world—and that in Him the world in its totality has become again a *liturgy,* a *communion,* an *ascension.* To *accept* secularism as the *truth* about the world is, therefore, to change the original Christian faith so deeply and so radically, that the question must be asked: do we really speak of the same Christ?

3

The only purpose of this book has been to show, or rather to "signify" that the choice between these two reductions of Christianity—to "religion" and to "secularism"—is not the only choice, that in fact it is a false dilemma. "And ye are witnesses to these things. . . ." To what things? In a language that can never be adequate, we have tried to speak about them. And it is our certitude that in the ascension of the Church in Christ, in the joy of the world to come, in the Church as the *sacrament*—the gift, the beginning, the presence, the promise, the reality, the anticipation—of the Kingdom, is the source and the beginning of all Christian mission. It is only as we return from the light and the joy of Christ's presence that we recover the world as a meaningful field of our Christian action, that we see the true reality of the world and thus discover what we must do. Christian mission is always at its beginning. It is today that I am sent back into the world *in joy and peace,* "having seen the true light," having partaken of the Holy Spirit, having been a witness of divine Love.

What am I going to do? What are the Church and each Christian to do in this world? What is our *mission?*

To these questions there exist no answers in the form of practical "recipes." "It all depends" on thousands of factors —and, to be sure, all faculties of our human intelligence and wisdom, organization and planning, are to be constantly used. Yet—and this is the one "point" we wanted to make in these pages—"it all depends" primarily on our being real witnesses to the joy and peace of the Holy Spirit, to that new life of which we are made partakers in the Church. The Church is the sacrament of the Kingdom —not because she possesses divinely instituted acts called "sacraments," but because first of all she is the possibility given to man to see in and through this world the "world to come," to see and to "live" it in Christ. It is only when in the darkness of *this world* we discern that Christ has already "filled all things with Himself" that these *things,* whatever they may be, are revealed and given to us full of meaning and beauty. A Christian is the one who, wherever he looks, finds Christ and rejoices in Him. And this joy *transforms* all his human plans and programs, decisions and actions, making all his mission the sacrament of the world's return to Him who is the life of the world.

APPENDICES

1

*Worship in A Secular Age**

"Tout est ailleurs."
—JULIEN GREEN

To put together—in order to relate them to one another—the terms *worship* and *secular age,* seems to presuppose that we have a clear understanding of both of them, that we know the realities they denote, and that we thus operate on solid and thoroughly explored grounds. But is this really the case? I begin my paper with a question mainly because I am convinced that in spite of today's generalized preoccupation with "semantics," there is a great deal of confusion about the exact meaning of the very terms we use in this discussion.

Not only among Christians in general, but even among the Orthodox themselves there exists in fact no consensus, no commonly accepted frame of reference concerning either *worship* or *secularism,* and thus *a fortiori* the problem of their interrelation. Therefore my paper is an attempt not so much to solve the problem as to clarify it, and to do this if possible within a consistent Orthodox perspective. In my opinion, the Orthodox, when discussing the problems

*Paper read at the Eighth General Assembly of SYNDESMOS, on July 20, 1971, at Hellenic College, Brookline, Mass. Published first in *St. Vladimir's Theological Quarterly,* Vol. 16, No. 1 (1972).

stemming from our present "situations," accept them much too easily in their Western formulations. They do not seem to realize that the Orthodox tradition provides above all a possibility, and thus a necessity, of reformulating these very problems, of placing them in a context whose absence or deformation in the Western religious mind may have been the root of so many of our modern "impasses." And as I see it, nowhere is this task more urgently needed than in the range of problems related to *secularism* and proper to our so-called *secular age*.

2

Secularism has been analysed, described, and defined in these recent years in a great variety of ways, but to the best of my knowledge none of these descriptions has stressed a point which I consider to be essential and which reveals indeed better than anything else the true nature of secularism, and thus can give our discussion its proper orientation.

Secularism, I submit, is above all a *negation of worship*. I stress:—not of God's existence, not of some kind of transcendence and therefore of some kind of religion. If secularism in theological terms is a heresy, it is primarily a heresy about man. It is the negation of man as a worshiping being, as *homo adorans*: the one for whom worship is the essential act which both "posits" his humanity and fulfills it. It is the rejection as ontologically and epistemologically "decisive," of the words which "always, everywhere and for all" were the true "epiphany" of man's relation to God, to the world and to himself: "It is meet and right to sing of Thee, to bless Thee, to praise Thee, to give thanks to Thee, and to worship Thee in every place of Thy dominion. . . ."

This definition of secularism most certainly needs explanation. For obviously it cannot be accepted by those, quite numerous today, who consciously or unconsciously reduce Christianity to either intellectual ("future of belief") or socio-ethical ("Christian service to the world") categories, and who therefore think that it must be possible to find not only some kind of accommodation, but even a deeper harmony between our "secular age" on the one hand, and worship on the other hand. If the proponents of what basically is nothing else but the Christian acceptance of secularism are right, then of course our whole problem is only that of finding or inventing a worship more acceptable, more "relevant" to the modern man's secular world view. And such indeed is the direction taken today by the great majority of liturgical reformers. What they seek is worship whose forms and content would "reflect" the needs and aspirations of the secular man, or even better, of secularism itself. For once more, secularism is by no means identical with atheism, and paradoxical as it may seem, can be shown to have always had a peculiar longing for a "liturgical" expression. If, however, my definition is right, then this whole search is a hopeless dead end, if not outright nonsense. Then the very formulation of our theme—"worship in a secular age"—reveals, first of all, an inner contradiction in terms, a contradiction which requires a radical reappraisal of the entire problem and its drastic reformulation.

3

To prove that my definition of secularism ("negation of worship") is correct, I must prove two points. One concerning worship: it must be proven that the very notion of worship implies a certain idea of man's relationship not only to God, but also to the world. And one concerning secularism: it must be proven that it is precisely this idea of worship that secularism explicity or implicitly rejects.

First let us consider worship. It is ironic but also quite revealing, it seems to me, of the present state of our theology, that the main "proof" here will be supplied not by theologians but by the *"Religionswissenschaft,"* that history and phenomenology of religions whose scientific study of worship, of both its forms and content, has been indeed virtually ignored by theologians. Yet even in its formative stage, when it had a strong anti-Christian bias, this *Religion-swissenschaft* seems to have known more about the nature and meaning of worship than the theologians who kept reducing sacraments to the categories of "form" and "matter," "causality," and "validity," and who in fact excluded the liturgical tradition from their theological speculations.

There can be no doubt however, that if, in the light of this by now methodologically mature phenomenology of religion, we consider worship in general and the Christian *leitourgia* in particular, we are bound to admit that the very principle on which they are built, and which determined and shaped their development, is that of the *sacramental* character of the world and of man's place in the world.

The term "sacramental" means here that the basic and primordial intuition which not only expresses itself in worship, but of which the entire worship is indeed the "phenomenon"—both effect and experience—is that the world, be it in its totality as cosmos, or in its life and becoming as time and history, is an *epiphany* of God, a means of His revelation, presence, and power. In other words, it not only "posits" the idea of God as a rationally acceptable cause of its existence, but truly "speaks" of Him and is in itself an essential means both of knowledge of God and communion with Him, and to be so is its true nature and its ultimate destiny. But then worship is truly an essential act, and man an essentially worshipping being, for it is *only* in worship that man has the source and the possibility of that knowledge which is communion, and of that communion which fulfills itself as true knowledge: knowledge of God and therefore knowledge of the world—communion with God and therefore communion with all that exists. Thus the very notion of worship is based on an intuition and experience of the world as an "epiphany" of God, thus the world—in worship—is revealed in its true nature and vocation as "sacrament."

And indeed, do I have to remind you of those realities, so humble, so "taken for granted" that they are hardly even mentioned in our highly sophisticated theological epistemologies and totally ignored in discussions about "hermeneutics," and on which nevertheless simply depends our very existence as Church, as *new creation,* as people of God and temple of the Holy Spirit? We *need* water and oil, bread and wine in order to be in communion with God and to know Him. Yet conversely—and such is the teaching, if not of our modern theological manuals, at least of the liturgy itself—it is this communion with God by means of "matter" that reveals the true meaning of "matter," i.e., of the world itself. We can only worship in time, yet it is worship that ultimately not only reveals the meaning of time, but truly "renews" time itself. There is no worship without the participation of the body, without words and silence, light and darkness, movement and stillness—yet it is in and through worship that all these essential expressions of man in his relation to the world are given their ultimate "term" of reference, revealed in their highest and deepest meaning.

Thus the term "sacramental" means that for the world to be means of worship and means of grace is not accidental, but the revelation of its meaning, the restoration of its essence, the fulfillment of its destiny. It is the "natural sacramentality" of the world that finds its expression in worship and makes the latter the essential ἔργον of man, the foundation and the spring of his life and activities as man. Being the epiphany of God, worship is thus the epiphany of the world; being communion with God, it is the only true communion with the world; being knowledge of God, it is the ultimate fulfillment of all human knowledge.

4

At this point, and before I come to my second point—secularism as negation of worship—one remark is necessary. If earlier I mentioned *Religionswissenschaft,* it is because this discipline establishes at is own level and according to its own methodology that such indeed is the nature and the meaning not only of Christian worship, but of worship "in general," of worship as a primordial and universal phenomenon. A Christian theologian, however, ought to concede, it seems to me, that this is especially true of the Christian *leitourgia* whose uniqueness lies in its stemming from the faith in the Incarnation, from the great and all-embracing mystery of the "Logos made flesh." It is indeed extremely important for us to remember that the uniqueness, the *newness* of Christian worship is not that it has no *continuity* with worshop "in general," as some overly zealous apologists tried to prove at the time when *Religion-swissenschaf* simply reduced Christianity and its worship to pagan mystery-cults, but that in Christ this very continuity is fulfilled, receives its ultimate and truly new significance so as to truly bring all "natural" worship to an end. Christ is the fulfillment of worship as adoration and prayer, thanksgiving and sacrifice, communion and knowledge, because He is the ultimate "epiphany" of man as worshiping being, the fulness of God's manifestation and presence by means of the world. He is the true and full Sacrament because He is the fulfillment of the world's essential "sacramentality."

If, however, this "continuity" of the Christian *leitourgia* with the whole of man's worship includes in itself an equally essential principle of *discontinuity,* if Christian worship being the fulfillment and the end of all worship is at the same time a *beginning,* a radically *new* worship, it is not because of any ontological impossibility for the world to be the sacrament of Christ. No, it is because the world rejected Christ by killing Him, and by doing so rejected its own destiny and fulfillment. Therefore, if the basis of all Christian worship is the Incarnation, its true content is always the Cross and the Resurrection. Through these events the new life in Christ, the Incarnate Lord, is "hid with Christ in God," and made into a life "not of this world." The world which rejected Christ must itself die in man if it is to become again means of communion, means of participation in the life which shone forth from the grave, in the Kingdom which is not "of this world," and which in terms of this world is still to come.

And thus the bread and wine—the food, the matter,

the very symbol of this world and therefore the very content of our *prosphora* to God, to be changed into the Body and Blood of Christ and become the communion to His Kingdom—must in the *anaphora* be "lifted up," taken out of "this world." And it is only when the Church in the Eucharist leaves this world and ascends to Christ's table at His Kingdom, that she truly sees and proclaims heaven and earth to be full of His glory and God as having "filled all things with Himself." Yet, once more this "discontinuity," this vision of all things as new, is possible only because at first there is continuity and not negation, because the Holy Spirit makes "all things new" and not "new things." It is because all Christian worship is always *remembrance* of Christ "in the flesh" that it can also be remembrance, i.e., expectation and anticipation, of His Kingdom. It is only because the Church's *leitourgia* is always cosmic, i.e., assumes into Christ all creation, and is always historical, i.e. assumes into Christ all time, that it can therefore also be eschatological, i.e., make us true participants of the Kingdom to come.

Such then is the idea of man's relation to the world implied in the very notion of worship. Worship is by definition and act a reality with cosmic, historical, and eschatological dimensions, the expression thus not merely of "piety," but of an all-embracing "world view." And those few who have taken upon themselves the pain of studying worship in general, and Christian worship in particular, would certainly agree that on the levels of history and phenomenology at least, this notion of worship is objectively verifiable. Therefore, if today what people call worship are activities, projects, and undertakings having in reality nothing to do with this notion of worship, the responsibility for this lies with the deep semantic confusion typical of our confused time.

5

We can now come to my second point. Secularism, I said, is

above all a negation of worship. And indeed, if what we have said about worship is true, is it not equally true that secularism consists in the rejection, explicit or implicit, of precisely that idea of man and world which it is the very purpose of worship to express and communicate?

This rejection, moreover, is at the very foundation of secularism and constitutes its inner criterion, but as I have already said, secularism is by no means identical to atheism. A modern secularist quite often accepts the idea of God. What, however, he emphatically negates is precisely the sacramentality of man and world. A secularist views the world as containing within itself its meaning and the principles of knowledge and action. He may deduce meaning from God and ascribe to God the origin of the world and the laws which govern it. He may even admit without difficulty the possibility of God's intervention in the world's existence. He may believe in survival after death and the immortality of the soul. He may relate to God his ultimate aspirations, such as a just society and the freedom and equality of all men. In other words, he may "refer" his secularism to God and make it "religious"—the object of ecclesiastical programs and ecumenical projects, the theme of Church assemblies and the subject matter of "theology." All this changes nothing in the fundamental "secularity" of his vision of man and world, in the world being understood, experienced, and acted upon in its own immanent terms and for its own immanent sake. All this changes nothing in his fundamental rejection of "epiphany": the primordial intuition that everything in this world and the world itself not only have *elsewhere* the cause and principle of their existence, but are *themselves* the manifestation and presence of that *elsewhere,* and that this is indeed the life of their life, so that disconnected from that "epiphany" all is only darkness, absurdity, and death.

And nowhere is this essence of secularism as negation of worship better revealed than in the secularist's dealing with worship. For paradoxical as it may sound, the secularist in a way is truly obsessed with worship. The "acme" of religious secularism in the West—Masonry—is made up almost entirely of highly elaborated ceremonies saturated with "symbolism." The recent prophet of the "secular city," Harvey Cox, felt the need to follow up his first best-seller with a book on "celebration." Celebration is in fact very fashionable today. The reasons for this seemingly peculiar phenomenon are in reality quite simple. They not only do not invalidate, but on the contrary confirm my point. For on the one hand, this phenomenon proves that whatever the degree of his secularism or even atheism, man remains essentially a "worshiping being," forever nostalgic for rites and rituals no matter how empty and artificial is the ersatz offered to him. And on the other hand, by proving the inability of secularism to create genuine worship, this phenomenon reveals secularism's ultimate and tragic incompatibility with the essential Christian world view.

Such inability can be seen, in the first place, in the secularist's very approach to worship, in his naive conviction that worship, as everything else in the world, can be a rational construction, the result of planning, "exchange of views," and discussions. Quite typical of this are the very fashionable discussions of new symbols, as if symbols could be, so to speak, "manufactured," brought into existence through committee deliberations. But the whole point here is that the secularist is constitutionally unable to see in symbols anything but "audio-visual aids" for communicating ideas. Last winter a group of students and teachers of a well-known seminary spent a semester "working" on a "liturgy" centered on the following "themes": the S.S.T., ecology, and the flood in Pakistan. No doubt they "meant well." It is their presuppositions which are wrong: that the traditional worship can have no "relevance" to these themes and has nothing to reveal about them, and that unless a "theme" is somehow clearly spelled out in the liturgy, or made into its "focus," it is obviously outside the spiritual reach of liturgical experience. The secularist is very fond today of terms such as "symbolism," "sacrament," "transformation," "celebration," and of the entire panoply of cultic terminology. What he does not realize, however, is that the use he makes of them reveals, in fact, the death of symbols and the decomposition of the sacrament. And he does not realize this because in his rejection of the world's and man's sacramentality he is reduced to viewing symbols as indeed mere illustrations of ideas and concepts, which they emphatically are not. There can be no celebration of ideas and concepts, be they "peace," "justice," or even "God." The Eucharist is not a symbol of friendship, togetherness, or any other state of activity however desirable. A vigil or a fast are, to be sure, "symbolic": they always express, manifest, fulfill the Church as expectation, they are themselves that expectation and preparation. To make them into "symbols" of political protest or ideological affirmation, to use them as means to that which is not their "end," to think that the liturgical symbols can be used arbitrarily—is to signify the death of worship, and this in spite of the obvious success and popularity of all these "experiments."

To anyone who has had, be it only once, the true experience of worship, all this is revealed immediately as the ersatz it is. He knows that the secularist's worship of relevance is simply incompatible with the true relevance of worship. And it is here, in this miserable liturgical failure, whose appalling results we are only beginning to see, that secularism reveals its ultimate religious emptiness and, I will not hesitate to say, its utterly anti-Christian essence.

6

Does all this mean a simple dismissal of our very theme: "worship in a secular age"? Does this mean that there is nothing we, as Orthodox, can do in this secular age except to perform on Sunday our "ancient and colorful" rites, and to live from Monday until Saturday a perfectly "secularized" life, sharing in a world view which is in no way related to these rites?

To this question my answer is an emphatic *No.* I am

convinced that to accept this "coexistence,"[1] as is advocated today by many seemingly well-intentioned Christians, would not only mean a betrayal of our own faith, but that sooner or later, and probably sooner than later, it would lead to the disintegration of precisely that which we want to preserve and perpetuate. I am convinced, moreover, that such a disintegration has already begun and is concealed only by the grace-proof walls of our ecclesiastical "establishments" (busy as they are in defending their ancient rights and privileges and primacies and condemning one another as "noncanonical"), peaceful rectories, and self-righteous pieties. To this latter we shall return a little later.

What we have to understand first of all, is that the problem under discussion is complicated by something our well-intentioned "conservatives" do not comprehend, in spite of all their denouncing and condemning of secularism. It is the fact of the very real connection between secularism —its origin and its development—and Christianity. Secularism —we must again and again stress this—is a "stepchild" of Christianity, as are, in the last analysis, all secular ideologies which today dominate the world—not, as it is claimed by the Western apostles of a Christian acceptance of secularism, a legitimate child, but a *heresy*. Heresy, however, is always the distortion, the exaggeration, and therefore the mutilation of something true, the affirmation of one "choice" (*aizesis* means choice in Greek), one element at the expence of the others, the breaking up of the catholicity of Truth. But then heresy is also always a question addressed to the Church, and which requires, in order to be answered, an effort of Christian thought and conscience. To condemn a heresy is relatively easy. What is much more difficult

---

[1]Nowhere better seen than in the classical argument of the partisans of the "old calendar": on December 25th we can fully share in the "secularized" Western Christmas with its Christmas trees, family reunions, and exchange of gifts, and then on January 7th we have the "true"—religious—Christmas. The tenants of this view do not realize, of course, that had the early Church shared in such an understanding of her relation to the world, she would have never instituted Christmas, whose purpose was precisely to "exorcize," transform, and Christianize an existing pagan festival.

is to *detect* the question it implies, and to give this question
an adequate answer. Such, however, was always the Church's
dealing with "heresies"—they always provoked an effort of
creativity within the Church so that the condemnation
became ultimately a widening and deepening of Christian
faith itself. To fight Arianism St. Athanasius advocated
the term *consubstantial,* which earlier, and within a different theological context, was condemned as heretical. Because of this he was violently opposed, not only by Arians
but by "conservatives," who saw in him an innovator and a
"modernist." Ultimately, however, it became clear that it
was he who saved Orthodoxy, and that the blind "conservatives" consciously or unconsciously helped the Arians.
Thus, if secularism is, as I am convinced, the great *heresy*
of our own time, it requires from the Church not mere
anathemas, and certainly not compromises, but above all
an effort of understanding so it may ultimately be overcome
by truth.

The uniqueness of secularism, its difference from the
great heresies of the patristic age, is that the latter were
provoked by the encounter of Christianity with Hellenism,
whereas the former is the result of a "breakdown" within
Christianity itself, of its own deep metamorphosis. The
lack of time prevents me from dealing with this point in
detail. I shall limit myself therefore to one "symbolic" example directly related to our theme.[2] At the end of the
twelfth century a Latin theologian, Berengarius of Tours,
was condemned for his teaching on the Eucharist. He maintained that because the presence of Christ in the eucharistic
elements is "mystical" or "symbolic," it is not *real.* The
Lateran Council which condemned him—and here is for
me the crux of the matter—simply reversed the formula.
It proclaimed that since Christ's presence in the Eucharist
is *real,* it is not "mystical." What is truly decisive here is
precisely the disconnection and the opposition of the two
terms *verum* and *mystice,* the acceptance, on both sides,

---

[2]For a fuller treatment of this point see Appendix II: "Sacrament
and Symbol."

that they are mutually exclusive. Western theology thus declared that that which is "mystical" or "symbolic" is not real, whereas that which is "real" is not symbolic. This was, in fact, the collapse of the fundamental Christian *mysterion,* the antinomical "holding together" of the reality of the symbol, and of the symbolism of reality. It was the collapse of the fundamental Christian understanding of creation in terms of its ontological *sacramentality.* And since then, Christian thought, in Scholasticism and beyond it, never ceased to oppose these terms, to reject, implicitly or explicitly, the "symbolic realism" and the "realistic symbolism" of the Christian world view. "As if God did not exist"—this formula originated not with Bonhoeffer or any modern apostle of "religionless Christianity." It is indeed implied already in Thomism, with its basic epistemological distinction between *causa prima* and *causae secundae.* Here is the real cause of *secularism,* which is ultimately nothing else but the affirmation of the world's autonomy, of its self-sufficiency in terms of reason, knowledge, and action. The downfall of Christian symbolism led to the dichotomy of the "natural" and the "supernatural" as the only framework of Christian thought and experience. And whether the "natural" and the "supernatural" are somehow related to one another by *analogia entis,* as in Latin theology, or whether this analogy is totally rejected, as in Barthianism, ultimately makes no difference. In both views the world ceases to be the "natural" sacrament of God, and the supernatural sacrament to have any "continuity" with the world.

Let us not be mistaken, however. This Western theological framework was in fact accepted by the Orthodox East also, and since the end of the patristic age our theology has been indeed much more "Western" than "Eastern." If secularism can be properly termed a Western heresy, the very fruit of the basic Western "deviation," our own scholastic theology has also been permeated with it for centuries, and this in spite of violent denunciations of Rome and papism. And it is indeed ironic, but not at all accidental, that psychologically the most "Western" among the Orthodox today are precisely the ultra-conservative "Super-

Orthodox," whose whole frame of mind is legalistic and syllogistic on the one hand, and is made up, on the other hand, of those very "dichotomies" whose introduction into Christian thought is the "original sin" of the West. Once these dichotomies are accepted, it does not matter, theologically speaking, whether one "accepts" the world, as in the case of the Western enthusiast of "secular Christianity," or "rejects" it, as in the case of the "Super-Orthodox" prophet of apocalyptic doom. The optimistic positivism of the one, and the pessimistic negativism of the other are, in fact, two sides of the same coin. Both, by denying the world its natural "sacramentality" and radically opposing the "natural" to the "supernatural," make the world *grace-proof*, and ultimately lead to *secularism*. And it is here, within this spiritual and psychological context, that the problem of worship in relation to modern secularism acquires its real significance.

7

For it is clear that this deeply "Westernized" theology has had a very serious impact on worship, or rather, on the experience and comprehension of worship, on that which elsewhere I have defined as liturgical piety.[8] And it has had this impact because it satisfied a deep desire of man for a legalistic religion that would fulfill his need for both the "sacred"—a divine sanction and guarantee—and the "profane," i.e., a natural and secular life protected, as it were, from the constant challenge and absolute demands of God. It was a relapse into that religion which assures, by means of orderly transactions with the "sacred," security and clean conscience in this life, as well as reasonable rights to the "other world," a religion which Christ denounced by every word of His teaching, and which ultimately crucified Him. It is indeed much easier to live and to breathe within neat distinctions between the sacred and the profane, the

---

[8]See my *Introduction to Liturgical Theology* (London: Faith Press, 1966).

natural and the supernatural, the pure and the impure, to understand religion in terms of sacred "taboos," legal prescriptions and obligations, of ritual rectitude and canonical "validity." It is much more difficut to realize that such a religion not only does not constitute any threat to "secularism," but on the contrary, is its paradoxical ally.

And yet this is exactly what happened to our "liturgical piety," and not to worship as such—to its forms and structures, which were too traditional, too much a part of the Church's life to be altered in any substantial degree —but to our "comprehension" of these forms, to what *we* expect and therefore receive from worship. If worship as shaped by the liturgical tradition, the *lex orandi* of the Church, remained the same, its "comprehension" by the faithful became more and more determined by those very categories which the Orthodox liturgical tradition explicity and implicitly rejects by its every word, by its entire "ethos." And the deep tragedy here is that the imposition of these categories is accepted today to such an extent that any attempt to denounce them, to show their incompatibility with the true spirit and meaning of the *leitourgia,* is met by accusations of *modernism* and other mortal sins. And yet this is not a superficial verbal quarrel, not one of those academic storms which more often than not leave the Church undisturbed. This is truly a matter of life and death, because it is here and only here that the fightening heresy of secularism can find its proper Christian diagnosis and be defeated.

Lack of time compels me to limit myself to one example to show that the "dichotomies" mentioned above, which without any doubt have determined the deep metamorphosis of our liturgical piety, not only do not "connect" and relate one to another God, man, and the world, uniting them in one consistent world view, but on the contrary, abolish all "communications" and "correspondences" between them.

Thus, for example, to bless water, making it "holy water," may have two entirely different meanings. It may mean, on the one hand, the transformation of something *profane,* and thus religiously void or neutral, into something *sacred,* in which case the main religious meaning of "holy water" is precisely that it is no longer "mere" water, and is in fact opposed to it—as the sacred is to the profane. Here the act of blessing reveals nothing about water, and thus about matter or world, but on the contrary makes them irrelevant to the new function of water as "holy water." The sacred posits the profane as precisely profane, i.e., religiously meaningless.

On the other hand, the same act of blessing may mean the revelation of the true "nature" and "destiny" of water, and thus of the world—it may be the epiphany and the fulfillment of their "sacramentality." By being restored through the blessing to its proper function, the "holy water" is revealed as the true, full, adequate water, and matter becomes again means of communion with and knowledge of God.

Now anyone who is acquainted with the content and the text of the great prayer of blessing of water—at Baptism and Epiphany—knows without any doubt that they belong to the second of the two meanings mentioned above, that their term of reference is not the dichotomy of the sacred and the profane, but the "sacramental" potentiality of creation in its totality, as well as in each of its elements. Yet anyone who is acquainted with our liturgical piety— in this case the "comprehension" by the immense majority of the faithful of the meaning of "holy water"—knows equally well that it is the first meaning which triumphs here to the virtual exclusion of the second one. And the same analysis can be applied, with the same results, to practically every aspect of worship: to sacraments, to the liturgy of time, to heortology, etc. "Sacramentality" has been replaced everywhere by "sacrality," "epiphany" by an almost magical incrustation into time and matter (the "natural"), by the "supernatural."

What is truly disturbing here is that such liturgical piety, such understanding and experience of worship, not only is in no way a challenge to secularism, but is in fact one of its very sources. For it leaves the world profane, i.e., precisely *secular,* in the deepest sense of this term: as totally incapable of any real communication with the Divine, of any real transformation and transfiguration. Having nothing to reveal about world and matter, about time and nature, this idea and this experience of worship "disturb" nothing, question nothing, challenge nothing, are indeed "applicable" to nothing. They can therefore peacefully "coexist" with any secular ideology, any form of secularism. And there is virtually no difference here between liturgical "rigorists," i.e., those who stress long services, compliance with rubrics and the Typicon, and liturgical "liberals," always ready and anxious to shorten, adapt, and adjust. For in both cases what is denied is simply the *continuity* between "religion" and "life," the very function of worship as power of transformation, judgment, and change. Again, paradoxically and tragically, this type of approach towards worship and this kind of liturgical experience are indeed the source and the support of secularism.

8

And this at a time when secularism begins to "crack" from inside! If my reading of the great confusion of our time is correct, this confusion is, first of all, a deep crisis of secularism. And it is truly ironic, in my opinion, that so many Christians are seeking some accommodation with secularism precisely at the moment when it is revealing itself to be an untenable spiritual position. More and more signs point toward one fact of paramount importance: the famous "modern man" is already looking for a path beyond secularism, is again thirsty and hungry for "something else." Much too often this thirst and hunger are satisfied not only by food of doubtful quality, but by artificial substitutes of all kinds. The spiritual confusion is at its peak. But is it not because the Church, because Christians themselves, have given up so easily that unique gift which they alone— and no one else!—could have given to the spiritually thirsty and hungry world of ours? Is it not because Christians, more than any others today, defend secularism and adjust to it

their very faith? Is it not because, having access to the true
mysterion of Christ, we prefer to offer to the world vague
and second-rate "social" and "political" advice? The world
is desperate in its need for Sacrament and Epiphany, while
Christians embrace empty and foolish worldly utopias.

My conclusions are simple. No, we do not need any *new*
worship that would somehow be more adequate to our
new secular world. What we need is a rediscovery of the
true meaning and power of worship, and this means of its
cosmic, ecclesiological, and eschatological dimensions and
content. This, to be sure, implies much work, much "cleaning
up." It implies study, education and effort. It implies giving
up much of that dead wood which we carry with us, seeing
in it much too often the very essence of our "traditions" and
"customs." But once we discover the true *lex orandi*, the
genuine meaning and power of our *leitourgia*, once it becomes
again the source of an all-embracing world view and the
power of living up to it—then and only then the unique
antidote to "secularism" shall be found. And there is nothing
more urgent today than this rediscovery, and this return—
not to the past—but to the light and life, to the truth and
grace that are eternally fulfilled by the Church when she
becomes—in her *leitourgia*—that which she is.

2

Sacrament and Symbol[1]

The initial difficulty encountered by an Orthodox when he speaks of sacraments lies in the necessity to choose between the various "strata" of his own theological tradition. If he opts for the more recent and official "theology of manuals" which developed in Orthodox theological schools since the sixteenth century, his presentation will undoubtedly be quite similar, in terminology as well as in content, to any Latin *De Sacramentis*. From a general definition of sacraments as "visible means of the invisible grace" he will proceed to the distinction in them between "form" and "matter," their institution by Christ, their numbering and classification and, finally, their proper administration as condition of their validity and efficacy[2]. It is a fact, however, which is recognized today by a growing number of Orthodox theologians, that this approach to sacraments, although accepted and taught for several centuries, has very little to do with the genuine tradition of the Eastern Church. It is seen rather as one of the most unfortunate results and expressions of the "pseudomorphosis" suffered by Orthodox theology after the breakdown of the patristic

---

[1]Published first in *Evangelium und Sacrament* (Strasburg: Oecumenica, 1970).

[2]See for example F. Gavin, *Some Aspects of Contemporary Greek Thought*: (London: SPCK, 1923), pp. 269—354, or Bishop Sylvester, *Opyit Pravoslavnogo Dogmaticheskogo Bogoslovia* (Orthodox Dogmatical Theology), Vol. IV, pp. 350—577, Vol. V, pp. 1—65 (Kiev: 1897).

age when tragic conditions of ecclesiastical life forced upon
Orthodox "intellectuals" a non-critical adoption of Western
theological categories and thought forms. The result was a
deeply "westernized" theology, whose tradition was maintained (and to some extent is still maintained) by theological
schools. In Russia, for example, theology was taught in
Latin until the forties of the nineteenth century! The
"Western captivity" of Orthodox theology has been
vigorously denounced by the best theologians of the last
hundred years and there exists today a significant movement aimed at the recovery by our theology of its own
genuine perspective and method.[3] The return to the Fathers,
to the liturgical and spiritual traditions which were virtually
ignored by the "theology of manuals," is beginning to bear
fruit. The process, however, is still in its initial stage, and
as to sacramental theology very little has been achieved,
which means that any effort of "recovery" and "reconstruction" here is of necessity a tentative and preliminary
one. The urgent task is precisely to recover a perspective,
to raise questions which within the antiquated framework
of "manuals" not only were not answered but could not
even be formulated.

2

What is "sacrament"? In answering this question the post-
patristic Western and "westernizing" theology places itself
within a mental context deeply, if not radically, different
from that of the early Church. I say *mental* and not intellectual because the difference belongs here to a level much
deeper than that of intellectual presuppositions or theological
terminology. Patristic theology, to be sure, was not less
"intellectual" than scholasticism, and as to terminology it
is precisely its unbroken continuity, the use of the same
words, however altered in their meaning, that may have

---

[3]On the history of that movement see G. Florovsky, *Puti Russkogo
Bogoslovija* (Ways of Russian Theology), (Paris: 1937).

concealed from too many historians of theology the discontinuity between the two types of sacramental theology.

Externally or formally this change consisted, first of all, in a new approach by sacramental theology to the very object of its study. In the early Church, in the writings of the Fathers, sacraments, inasmuch as they are given any systematic interpretation, are always explained in the context of their actual *liturgical* celebration, the explanation being, in fact, an exegesis of the liturgy itself in all its ritual complexity and concreteness. The medieval *De Sacramentis,* however, tends from its very inception to isolate the "sacrament" from its liturgical context, to find and to define in terms as precise as possible its *essence,* i. e., that which distinguishes it from the "non-sacrament." Sacrament in a way begins to be opposed to liturgy. It has, of course, its ritual expression, its "signum," which belongs to its essence, but this sign is viewed now as ontologically different from all other signs, symbols, and rites of the Church. And because of this difference, the precise sacramental sign alone is considered, to the exclusion of all other "liturgy," the proper object of theological attention. One can, for example, read and reread the elaborate treatment given in St. Thomas' *Summa* to sacraments without still knowing much about their liturgical celebration. And one can scrutinize virtually all Catholic and Orthodox treatises of Holy Orders without seeing mentioned, be it only once, the traditional and organic connection between ordination and Eucharist.[4] To historians of theology this change is due to what they describe as the progress of "scientific theology" and the growth of a "more precise" theological method.[5] In reality, however, this change, far from being a mere

---

[4]See Gavin, *ibid.,* pp. 370—378; Bishop Sylvester, *ibid.,* pp. 353—388.

[5]"The concept of sacrament-mysterion after having dominated for a long time sacramental theology had to fade away...It is certain that it made *a priori* impossible any precise analysis of the notion of sacrament... In fact, sacramental theology could make no progress as long as that notion was at its center"—A.M. Roguet, O.P., in St. Thomas d'Aquin, *Somme Theologique,* Les Sacrements (3a, Questions 60—65), (Paris: Desclee, 1945), p. 258.

"external" one, has its roots in a deep transformation of theological vision, indeed of the entire theological "world view." And it is the nature of that transformation that we must try to understand in the first place if we want to reach the initial meaning of the sacrament.

3

To simplify our task we can take as the starting point of this study the long and well-known debate which dominates from beginning to end the development in the West of sacramental and, more especially, eucharistic theology. It is the debate on the *real presence*. Nowhere indeed is better revealed the line dividing from one another the two approaches to the sacrament, as well as the reasons which led to the transformation of one into another. Within the context of that debate the term "real" clearly implies the possibility of another type of presence which therefore is *not* real. The term for that other presence in the Western intellectual and theological idiom is, we know, *symbolical.* We need not go here into the very complex and in many ways confused history of that term in Western thought.[6] It is clear that in the common theological language as it takes shape between the Carolingian renaissance and the Reformation, and in spite of all controversies between rival theological schools, the "incompatibility between symbol and reality," between "figura et veritas"[7] is consistently affirmed and accepted. "To the 'mystice, non vere' corresponds not less exclusively 'vere, non mystice.' "[8] The Fathers and the whole early tradition, however—and

---

[6]See W. Weidle, "Znak i Symbol" (Sign and Symbol), in *Bogoslovskaya Misl'* (Theological Thought), Essays published by the Orthodox Theological Institute in Paris (Paris: 1942), pp. 25—40, and E. Cassirer, *Philosophie der Symbolischen Formen,* I—III (1923 to 1929).

[7]B. Neunheuser, *Histoire des Dogmes: L'Eucharistie,* II. Au Moyen Age et a l'epoque moderne (Paris: Les Editions du Cerf, 1966), p. 42.

[8]H. de Lubac, *Corpus Mysticum: L'Eucharistie et l'Eglise au Moyen Age* (Paris: Aubier, 1944), p. 258.

we reach here the crux of the matter—not only do not know this distinction and opposition, but to them symbolism is the essential dimension of the sacrament, the proper key to its understanding. St. Maximus the Confessor, the sacramental theologian *par excellence* of the patristic age, calls the Body and Blood of Christ in the Eucharist *symbols* ("symbola"), *images* ("apeikonismata") and *mysteries* ("mysteria").[9] "Symbolical" here is not only not opposed to "real," but embodies it as its very expression and mode of manifestation. Historians of theology, in their ardent desire to maintain the myth of theological continuity and orderly "evolution," here again find their explanation in the "imprecision" of patristic terminology. They do not seem to realize that the Fathers' use of "symbolon" (and related terms) is not "vague" or "imprecise" but simply different from that of the later theologians, and that the subsequent transformation of these terms constitutes indeed the source of one of the greatest theological tragedies.

4

The difference here is primarily a difference in the apprehension of reality itself or, as we said above, a difference of "world view." If, for the Fathers, symbol is a key to sacrament it is because sacrament is in continuity with the symbolical structure of the world in which "omnes . . . creaturae sensibiles sunt signa rerum sacrum." And the world is symbolical—"signum rei sacrae"—in virtue of its being created by God; to be "symbolical" belongs thus to its ontology, the symbol being not only the way to perceive and understand reality, a means of cognition, but also a means of *participation*. It is then the "natural" symbolism of the world—one can almost say its "sacra-

---

[9]See R. Bornert, O.S.B., *Les Commentaires Byzantins de la Liturgie Byzantine du VII au XV siecle,* Archives de l'Orient Chretien, 9 (Paris: Institut Francais d'Etudes Byzantines), pp. 117f., and H. de Lubac, *Liturgie Cosmique* (Paris: Aubier, 1947), pp. 242f.

mentality"—that makes the sacrament *possible* and constitutes
the key to its understanding and apprehension. If the Christian sacrament is *unique,* it is not in the sense of being a
miraculous exception to the natural order of things created
by God and "proclaiming His glory." Its absolute newness
is not in its ontology as sacrament but in the specific "res"
which it "symbolizes," i. e., reveals, manifests, and communicates—which is Christ and His Kingdom. But even
this absolute newness is to be understood in terms not of
total discontinuity but in those of fulfillment. The "mysterion"
of Christ reveals and fulfills the ultimate meaning and
destiny of the world . itself. Therefore, the institution of
sacraments by Christ (a theme which will obsess the later
theology) is not the creation *ex nihilo* of the "sacramentality" itself, of the sacrament as means of cognition
and participation. In the words of Christ, "do *this* in
remembrance of me," the *this* (meal, thanksgiving,
breaking of bread) is already "sacramental."[10] The institution means that by being referred to Christ, "filled" with
Christ, the symbol is fulfilled and becomes *sacrament.*

5

It is this continuity of the sacrament with symbol that
the post-patristic theology begins, first, to minimize and
then simply to reject, and it does it because of a progressive
"dissolution" of the symbol, conditioned in turn by a new
concept of theology in its relation to faith. The ultimate
problem of all theology is that of *knowledge* and, more
precisely, of the possibility and nature of the knowledge
of God. If the Fathers hold together in a living and truly

---

[10]See for example F. L. Leenhardt on the pascal meal in Judaism:
". . . it appears as the sacrament of salvation. It evokes that which God
did and which He will achieve, the historical salvation and the eschatological
salvation. The notion of *zikkaron* . . . gives already a real basis to the idea
of sacrament"—*Le Sacrement de la Sainte Cene* (Neuchised Delachaux et
Nestle, 1948), p. 21, and also L. Bouyer, *Rite and Man: Natural Sacredness
and Christian Liturgy* (Notre Dame: University Press, 1967), pp. 63f.

"existential" synthesis, on the one hand, the absolute "other-ness" of God, the impossibility for creatures to know Him in His essence, and, on the other hand, the reality of man's communion with God, knowledge of God and "theosis," this synthesis is rooted primarily in their idea or rather intuition of the "mysterion" and of its mode of presence and operation—the symbol. For it is the very nature of symbol that it reveals and communicates the "other" *as* precisely the "other," the visibility of the invisible *as* invisible, the knowledge of the unknowable *as* unknowable, the presence of the future *as* future. The symbol is means of knowledge of that which cannot be known otherwise, for knowledge here depends on participation—the living encounter with and entrance into that "epiphany" of reality which the symbol is. But then theology is not only related to the "mysterion" but has in it its source, the condition of its very possibility. Theology as proper words and knowledge *about* God is the result of the knowledge *of* God—and in Him of all reality. The "original sin" of post-patristic theology consists therefore in the reduction of the concept of knowledge to rational or discursive knowl-edge or, in other terms, in the separation of knowledge from "mysterion". This theology does not reject the "symbol-ical world view" of the earlier tradition: the sentence quoted above—"omnes . . . sensibiles creaturae sunt signa rerum sacrum"—is from St. Thomas.[11] But it radically changes the understanding of that "signum." In the early tradition, and this is of paramount importance, the relationship be-tween the sign in the symbol (A) and that which it "signifies" (B) is neither a merely semantic one (A *means* B), nor causal (A *is the cause of* B), nor representative (A *represents* B). We called this relationship an *epiphany*. "A *is* B" means that the whole of A expresses, communicates, reveals, manifests the "reality" of B (although not neces-sarily the whole of it) without, however, losing its own ontological reality, without being dissolved in another "res."[12]

---

[11]*Summa Theologica,* Quest. 60, Art. 2,1.
[12]See Weidle, *ibid.*

But it was precisely this relationship between the A and the B, between the sign and the signified, that was changed. Because of the reduction of knowledge to rational or discursive knowledge there appears between A and B a *hiatus*. The symbol may still be means of knowledge but, as all knowledge, it is knowledge *about* and not knowledge *of*. It can be a revelation about the "res," but not the epiphany of the "res" itself. A can mean B, or represent it, or even, in certain instances, be the "cause" of its presence; but A is no longer viewed as the very means of "participation" *in* B. Knowledge and participation are now two different realities, two different orders.

6

For sacramental theology this "dissolution" of symbol had truly disastrous consequences. By changing the very notion of sacrament it radically transformed also that of theology, provoking finally a crisis whose real scope and depth we are beginning to realize only today. It must be clear by now, we hope, that the theme of "real presence" which we mentioned above and whose appearance in a way inaugurated the post-patristic period in sacramental theology was born out of theological doubt about the "reality" of symbol, i. e., its ability to contain and to communicate reality. We have briefly explained the reasons for that doubt: the identification, on the one hand, of symbol with means of knowledge, the reduction, on the other hand, of knowledge to rational and discursive knowledge *about,* rather than *of,* reality. And since tradition was unanimous in affirming the sacrament as *verum,* i. e., real, the question was bound to arise: how can the symbol be the vehicle or the mode of sacrament? Since, however, the patristic use of symbolical terminology in reference to sacraments was an equally obvious "datum" of the same tradition, the doubt was resolved at first by a mere reinforcement of one terminology—the "symbolical"—by another one—the "realistic." The sacrament is both "figura et res, veritas et figura," it is "non solum mystice sed etiam vere." But soon and in virtue of a progressive devaluation of symbol made inevitable by its dissolution, the two terms had to be viewed as not only different but, in fact, opposed to each other.[13] In the famous case of Berenger of Tours, the remarkable fact is the complete identity in the understanding of symbol between Berenger himself and those who condemned him. If for him the Body and Blood of Christ in the Eucharist are not real because they are symbolical, for the Council of Lateran of 1059 they are real precisely because they are not symbolical. The distinction having inevitably led to opposition, the latter has remained the fundamental framework of all subsequent theological development.[14]

7

There remained, however, the problem of the *signum* whose relation to the "res" of the sacrament had to be defined in a new way. For if it is not a symbol what is it? Post-patristic theology answered this question by defining *signum* as *cause*[15] and it is here that the notion and probably the experience of the sacrament suffered its deepest transformation. In the early tradition, the causality inherent in the sacrament, the sanctification it procures for those who partake of it, is inseparable from its symbolism for it is rooted in it. This in no way limits or contradicts the unique cause of all sacraments—their *institution* by Christ—for, as we have said already, the institution is precisely the fulfillment of a symbol by Christ and, therefore, its transformation into a sacrament. It is thus an act, not of discontinuity, but of fulfillment and actualization. It is the epiphany—in and through Christ—of the "new creation," not the creation of

---

[13]See H. de Lubac, *Corpus Mysticum*, Ch. 10 "Du Symbole a la Dialectique," pp. 255ff.

[14]Neunheuser, *ibid.*, pp. 46—55.

[15]E. Hugon, *La causalite instrumentale en theologie*, 2nd ed. (Paris: 1907).

something "new." And if it reveals the "continuity" between creation and Christ, it is because there exists, at first, a continuity between Christ and creation whose *logos,* life, and light He is. It is precisely this aspect of both the institution and sacrament that virtually disappear in post-patristic theology. The causality linking the institution to "signum" to "res" is viewed as extrinsic and formal, not as *intrinsic* and revealing. Rather than revealing through fulfillment, it guarantees the reality of the sacrament's *effect.* Even if, as in the case of the Eucharist, the sign is completely identified with reality, it is experienced in terms of the sign's annihilation rather than in those of fulfillment. In this sense the doctrine of transubstantiation, in its Tridentine form, is truly the collapse, or rather the suicide, of sacramental theology. If this new understanding of causality—as an extrinsic and formal guarantee—breaks the ontological continuity between the sign and the "res," it also rejects, *de facto,* all continuity between "institution" and the normal order of things. It is indeed *discontinuity* that is now being stressed and affirmed. Considered as the "causa principalis" of the "signum" as "causa secunda," institution becomes now an absolute starting point of a sacramental system entirely *sui generis.* And the efforts by some recent theologians to bring back into the notion of "signum" the "richness of traditional symbolism" concern the "accidents," not the "substance" in the doctrine and understanding of sacraments.

For doctrine and understanding are now very different from those of the early Church. In the latter, sacrament was not only "open" to, it truly "held together" the three dimensions or levels of the Christian vision of reality: those of the Church, the world, and the Kingdom. And "holding" them together it made them *known*—in the deepest patristic sense of the word knowledge—as both understanding and participation. It was the source of theology—knowledge *about* God in His relation to the world, the Church, and the Kingdom—because it was knowledge *of* God and, in Him, of all reality. Having its beginning, content and end in Christ, it at the same time revealed Christ as the beginning, the content and the end of all that which exists, as its Creator, Redeemer, and fulfillment. The transformation of the sacrament in post-patristic theology consisted, therefore, in its isolation within a self-contained and self-sufficient sacramental "organism." That external isolation of the sacrament from the liturgy which we mentioned before was, indeed, "symbolical" of a much deeper change. "The notion of the sacraments"—writes enthusiastically a contemporary theologian—"is something completely *sui generis* and the less anthropomorphism or even 'angelism' we introduce in it the better for theology . . . The sacraments have a mode of existence of their own, a psychology of their own, a grace of their own . . . In heaven and earth there is nothing comparable to sacraments."[16] It is when they were exalted and glorified as supreme *reality* that began the progressive alienation from them of theology, ecclesiology, and eschatology, an alienation which—whether it is understood or not—is at the origin of today's crisis, the source and the poison of "secularism" . . . As means of individual piety and sanctification they preserved all their "value." As catholic acts of the Church fulfilling herself, as symbols in "this world" of "the world to come," of the consummation in God of all things—they were simply forgotten.

8

We can return now to the Orthodox "perspective." The preceding analysis is meant to prove one thing: if that perspective is to be recovered it can only be through the rediscovery of those dimensions of *sacrament* which have been either obscured or simply ignored during the long dependence of Orthodox theology on Western, mainly Latin, systems and thought forms. How is this rediscovery to be made? It certainly cannot be a merely "intellectual" one. A mere reading of the Fathers, useful and essential as it is,

---

[16]Dom Vonier, *La Clef de la Doctrine Eucharistique,* trans. P. Roguet (Paris: Les Editions du Cerf [no date]).

will not suffice. For even patristic texts can be made, and are often made, into "proofs" of theological systems deeply alien to the real "mind" of the Fathers. The "patristic revival" of our time would miss completely its purpose if it were to result in a rigid "patristic system" which in reality never existed. It is indeed the eternal merit of the Fathers that they showed the dynamic and not static nature of Christian theology, its power always to be "contemporary" without reduction to any "contemporaneousness," open to all human aspirations without being determined by any of them. If the return to the Fathers were to mean a purely formal repetition of their terms and formulations, it would be as wrong and as useless as the discarding of the Fathers by "modern" theology because of their presumably "antiquated" world view.

All this applies, first of all, to our use of the term "symbol." If it is deliberately posited here as the center of sacramental theology and as a key to its "reconstruction," it is not simply because we find it in patristic texts. For we find in these texts many other terms equally, if not more, important for their understanding. And it would be easy, on the one hand, to prove that, from a purely terminological point of view, the term symbol is neither the most frequent, nor the most essential one, and, on the other hand, that no word in patristic texts is "absolute" in itself, but each receives its meaning, its theological "semantics" only within a wider theological and spiritual context. What proves then that the selection of this term, in preference to all others, is justified and that our understanding of it is correct? Was it not interpreted already by scholastic theology and in a sense which is held here to be erroneous?

To all these questions the answer is that, even if the Fathers had not used this word as such at all, it would have still been for us today the most adequate means to rediscover the meaning of that fundamental experience to which their writings bear testimony, to which all of them—explicitly or implicitly—refer, and which alone ultimately interests us in the Fathers. For it is this word, or rather the meaning which it acquires today more and more, that constitutes the best it not the unique bridge between, on the one hand, the experience and the world view of the Fathers and, on the other hand, the deepest aspirations, doubts, and confusions of our age, whether it is labeled "modern," "secular," or "technological." It is indeed this term *symbol* that emerges today as the "focus," the central preoccupation of both religious and secular thought, as the preliminary question on which all other questions depend, as the very "symbol" of man's confusion and search. If today one so often hears about the need for "new symbols," if symbol and symbolism are the objects of study and curiosity in circles which otherwise have nothing in common, it is because the basic experience behind all this is that of a complete disruption and breakdown in "communication," of the tragic lack of a "unitive principle" which would have the power to bring together and to hold together again the broken and atomized facets of human existence and knowledge. And it is this unitive principle, whose absence is felt so strongly and the search for which dominates modern thought, that is given the name *symbol*. Its connotations are both cognitive and participatory, for its function is to reunify knowledge as well as existence by reuniting them one with another. One does not know *what* this symbol is, but that which one *hopes for* from it is indeed much closer to the patristic idea and experience of symbol than those of the post-patristic age, and this is why we call it a bridge."[17]

9

The Christian, however, by definition ought to *know*. Does he not confess Christ to be both the *light* and the *life* of the world, the fulfillment of all knowledge and the redeemer

---

[17]See for further observations such books as: R. C. Zachner, *Matter and Spirit* (New York: Harper and Row, 1963); M. Eliade, *Mephistopheles and the Androgyne: Studies in Religious Myth and Symbol* (New York, Sheed and Ward, 1965); T. J. J. Altizer, *Mircea Eliade and the Dialectic of the Sacred* (Philadelphia, The Westminster Press, 1963); K. Jaspers, *Truth and Symbol* (New York, Twayne Publ., 1959).

of all existence? In terms just described and which are the
very terms of the world's search for "symbol"—is He not
indeed the Symbol of all symbols? Was it not said by
Christ Himself that the one who sees Him sees the Father,
the one who is in Him has the communion of the Holy
Spirit, the one who believes in Him has already—here and
now—eternal life? But why then does not the Christian
faith seem to be either seen or accepted by the world as
the fulfillment of its search for the symbol, and seems so
"irrelevant" to it? It is at this point, in this agonizing
"focus" of the actual Christian situation, that the preceding
analysis acquires, we hope, its true significance. For it shows
that if Christianity fails to fulfill its symbolic function—to
be that "unitive principle"—it is because "symbol" was
broken, at first, by Christians themselves. As a result of this
breakdown Christianity has come to look today, in the eyes
of the world at least, like, on the one hand, a mere intellectual
doctrine which moreover "cracks" under the pressure of an
entirely different intellectual context, or, on the other hand,
a mere religious institution which also "cracks" under the
pressure of its own institutionalism. And it is certainly not
the adjective "holy" apposed to that doctrine and to that
institution that will by itself overcome the "credibility gap"
and make Christianity the symbol it ceased to be. For the
whole point is that *holy* is not and can never be a mere
adjective, a definition sufficient to quarantee the divine
authority and origin of anything. If it defines anything
it is from inside, not outside. It reveals and manifests, *vide*
Rudolf Otto, the "mysterium tremendum," i.e., an inherent
power which in a doctrine transcends its intellectualism
and in an institution its institutionalism. It is this "holy"—
the power of an epiphany—that is hopelessly missing today
in both doctrine and institution, and this, not because of
human sins and limitations, but precisely because of a
deliberate choice: the rejection and the dissolution of *symbol*
as the fundamental structure of Christian "doctrine" and
Christian "institution."

The situation is not relieved in the least by the many
"modern" Christians, even theologians, who join the others

in crying for "new symbols" and who think that Christianity will recover its "relevance" for the world if only Christ could be shown to be the "symbol" of this or of that, the "illustration" of an ideology, the "image" and the "personification" of an attitude. They hopelessly remain prisoners of that same—extrinsic and illustrative—notion of the symbol which their predecessors invented and which serves today as a *postfactum* justification for their surrender to ideologies and attitudes whose connection to Christ is, to say the least, debatable. They hopelessly do not understand that for Christ to be "symbol" of anything in the world, the world itself must, in the first place, be known, viewed and experienced as the "symbol" of God, as the epiphany of His holiness, power and glory—that, in other terms, it is not "Christ" or "God" that have to be explained in terms of this world and of its passing needs so as to become their "symbols" but, on the contrary, it is God and God alone that has made this world His symbol, has then fulfilled this symbol in Christ and will consummate it in His eternal Kingdom. When deprived of this symbol the world becomes chaos and destruction, idol and error, and it is condemned to disappear, for the very nature of its "schema" (image, fashion) is to "pass away" (I Cor. 7:31). To make Christ the symbol of this passing world is the ultimate in foolishness and blindness, for He came to perform exactly the opposite—to save the world by restoring it as the "symbol" of God, as thirst and hunger for fulfillment in God, as "signum" of and passage into His Kingdom. And He saved it by destroying its self-sufficiency and opaqueness, by revealing in "this world" the Church—the symbol of the "new creation" and the sacrament of the "world to come."

And if Christians want, as they claim and as indeed they must, to serve the world, to supply it again with the "symbol" which it so desperately seeks, they can achieve it only if they themselves rediscover that symbol and rediscover it there where it has always been—by divine will and institution—in the Church. The Fathers or tradition can help them in this rediscovery, can purify their vision, "explain" in a way how it is to be made; they cannot be that rediscovery itself. And thus the last question remains: where and how can it be achieved?

10

The answer of Orthodox theology once it recovers from its "Western captivity" ought to be: in the unbroken liturgical life of the Church, in that sacramental tradition which in the East, at least, has not been significantly altered by the wanderings of an alienated theology. We have pointed out already that the fatal error of post-patristic rationalism was the isolation of the sacrament from the liturgy as total expression of the Church's life and faith. It meant, in fact, the isolation of the sacrament from the symbol, i.e., from that connection and communication with the whole of reality which are fulfilled in the sacrament. By becoming a closed and self-contained "means of grace," a drop of reality in a sea of symbols, the sacrament deprived the liturgy of its proper function—to connect the sacrament with the Church, the world, and the Kingdom, or, in other terms, with its ecclesiological, cosmical and eschatological content and dimension. The liturgy was left to "piety" which adorned it with thousands of explanations and interpretations, "symbolical" this time in the new "illustrative" and nominal meaning of that word. Whether viewed "archeologically"—as a collection of "ancient and colorful" rites, or "pictorially"—as a kind of audio-visual support for prayer, it indeed became *irrelevant*—to theology, to mission, and, in brief, to the total life of the Church. It keeps and probably will always keep its faithful—the "liturgically minded" Christians. But to the Church at large, to the "activists" as well as "gnostics," it seems to offer nothing.

To rediscover the initial and organic unity between the liturgy and the sacrament, the liturgy through the sacrament and the sacrament through the liturgy, as one dynamic reality in which *symbol*—the liturgy—is always fulfilled in the *sacrament*—such then is the condition for the recovery of that perspective which alone can lead us beyond the dead-ends of our present situation. And it is indeed the liturgical nature of the sacrament as well as the sacramental nature of liturgy and, through it, of the Church herself that are the living sources of that dynamic synthesis of which the Fathers remain the eternal witness. But that synthesis is not only in the past and in the books. It is with us—here and now— if we have eyes to see and ears to hear, if putting aside the wrong problems accumulated throughout centuries we can reach the reality of the Church and understand again the "lex orandi" as the source of her "lex credendi."

It is at this point that the real task, implied in the theme of this article, ought to begin. For it consists in *showing*, on the basis of a detailed study of the "leitourgia," the liturgical tradition and experience of the Church, the true content of that *Symbol* which the Church is and which she fulfills in the *Sacrament*, thus fulfilling herself. To show and to prove this is obviously impossible within the scope of this essay which remains therefore a very general introduction, a preliminary indication of a possible perspective. In concluding, we can only say that if such a task were undertaken, it would show that the proper function of the "leitourgia" has always been to *bring together*, within one symbol, the three levels of the Christian faith and life: the Church, the world, and the Kingdom; that the Church herself is thus the sacrament in which the broken, yet still "symbolical," life of "this world" is brought, in Christ and by Christ, into the dimension of the Kingdom of God, becoming itself the sacrament of the "world to come," or that which God has from all eternity prepared for those who love Him, and where all that which is human can be transfigured by grace so that all things may be consummated in God; that finally it is here and only here—in the "mysterion" of God's presence and action—that the Church always becomes that which she is: the Body of Christ and the Temple of the Holy Spirit, the unique *Symbol* "bringing together"—by bringing to God the world for the life of which He gave His Son.